Toxic Magnetism
How and why EMPATHS attract NARCISSISTS
by KARA LAWRENCE

Toxic Magnetism

Kara Lawrence

Published by Kara Lawrence, 2019.

While every precaution has been taken in the preparation of this book, the publisher assumes no responsibility for errors or omissions, or for damages resulting from the use of the information contained herein.

TOXIC MAGNETISM

First edition. September 8, 2019.

Copyright © 2019 Kara Lawrence.

Written by Kara Lawrence.

© **Copyright 2019 - All rights reserved.**

The content contained within this book may not be reproduced, duplicated or transmitted without direct written permission from the author or the publisher.

Under no circumstances will any blame or legal responsibility be held against the publisher, or author, for any damages, reparation, or monetary loss due to the information contained within this book, either directly or indirectly.

<u>Legal Notice:</u>

This book is copyright protected. It is only for personal use. You cannot amend, distribute, sell, use, quote or paraphrase any part, or the content within this book, without the consent of the author or publisher.

<u>Disclaimer Notice:</u>

Please note the information contained within this document is for educational and entertainment purposes only. All effort has been executed to present accurate, up to date, reliable, complete information. No warranties of any kind are declared or implied. Readers acknowledge that the author is not engaging in the rendering of legal, financial, medical or professional advice. The content within this book has been derived from various sources. Please consult a licensed professional before attempting any techniques outlined in this book.

By reading this document, the reader agrees that under no circumstances is the author responsible for any losses, direct or indirect, that are incurred as a result of the use of information contained within this document, including, but not limited to, errors, omissions, or inaccuracies.

Table of Contents

INTRODUCTION
   Chapter 1: 15 Warning Signs of a Toxic Relationship

   1. Let's Talk About Me
   2. They Turn Other People Against You
   3. They are Manipulative
   4. Fragmented Childhood
   5. They Seem Incredibly Charming…Maybe Too Charming
   6. The World "Love" Comes Out a Little Early
   7. They will Gaslight You
   8. Long-Term Friends Aren't on the List
   9. They Never Apologize
   10. You're Walking on Eggshells
   11. You Are Emotionally Drained
   12. You Need to Follow Strict Roles
   13. They Break You Down
   14. They Lie
   15. You Give More than You Get

   Chapter 2: What Is a Narcissist and How Do I Attract Them?

   Common Characteristics of a Narcissist
   Types of Narcissists
   Why Me?

Chapter 3: Toxic Puzzle Pieces: Complementary Characteristics of Empath and Narcissist

    Characteristics of an Empath
    Complementary Characteristics

Chapter 4: Empath to the Rescue! Why Do Women Often Want to "Fix" Men Showing Wounded Behavior?

    You Feel It's Your Mission
    You Can't Stand to See Anyone Hurting
    You Are Full of Love
    You Believe in Them
    You Are Nurturing
    You Believe You Are Their Life Savor

Chapter 5: Stages of a Toxic Relationship - Do You Relate?

    Stage One: The Attraction
    Stage Two: The First Red Flag
    Stage Three: Relationship Focuses on the Narcissist
    Stage Four: The Narcissist Has Control
    Stage Five: Empath Reaches a Breaking Point
    Stage Six: Plan to Escape
    Stage Seven: Healing

Chapter 6: Is My Partner An Energy Vampire? Take This Quiz

    Five Types of Energy Vampires

Questions:
Your Results

Chapter 7: What Is Codependency?

Signs of a Codependent Relationship
You Are In a Codependent Relationship, Now What?

Chapter 8: Setting Boundaries and Enforcing Them

Setting Boundaries
Enforcing Boundaries

Chapter 9: If I'm an Empath, Why Didn't I Sense a Narcissist?

How Strong Is Your Connection?
Your Need to Help Is Powerful
You Weren't Paying Attention to the Signs
You Didn't Understand Narcissism
But the Biggest Reason of Them All: Manipulation

Chapter 10: Escaping the Toxic Relationship and Recovering

Ending a Toxic Relationship
Finding the Courage to Leave
Steps to Healing

Chapter 11: Taking Preventative Measures

Do You Act Like Your Best Self In Their Presence?
How Do You Feel When You Are with Them?
Do They Open Up Your Creativity?
Learn From Your Mistakes
Getting Back Into the Right Mindset

Conclusion
References

Introduction

"EMPATHY IS ABOUT STANDING in someone else's shoes, feeling with his or her heart, seeing with his or her eyes. Not only is empathy hard to outsource and automate, but it makes the world a better place." - Daniel H. Pink (Walter, 2019).

Are you caught in an exhausting, repeated cycle of bad relationships that always turn out the same? Are you naturally giving and constantly find yourself being taken advantage of by chronic takers? Have you ever noticed that you attract the same type of person again and again and wonder why? Would you like to understand the elements that are driving this attraction and fueling this frustrating, toxic cycle? If you answered "yes" to any of these questions, keep reading!

There are many books offering help for recovery after a toxic relationship, but to date there are none that solely explore the root of the attraction that sensitive people and narcissists have for each other. Understanding why this pairing of personality types is almost irresistible for the parties involved is the only real way to guarantee hope for breaking the cycle and finally finding the healthy, satisfying, and reciprocal relationship that many of us yearn for but have been unable to find.

There was a time when I too was caught on what seemed like a broken record of bad, and often emotionally abusive, relationships. I saw friends with caring and giving partners who seemed happy in their mutually beneficial relationships, and they went on to long term commitments, but I seemed trapped in the repeated (and failed) experiment of trying to "fix" someone broken. I wondered why I was so subconsciously drawn to those who were clearly bad for me.

In this book, we will finally answer the question of why narcissists and sensitive people high in empathy are drawn so strongly toward each other. What are the psychological causes that constantly magnetize these two toward each other, and what are the deceptive tactics that the uncaring narcissist uses to hook the empath and keep them locked into the relationship? We will begin to understand with perfect clarity why chronic takers draw to natural givers, and how this feeding off one another can be completely draining for the sensitive.

Armed with the surprising truths I uncovered on the subject, and have now included in this book, I was finally able to keep an eye out for the warning signs of attraction that was exploitative, as opposed to loving. This allowed me to realize my true potential of using my unique gifts for the good of a relationship that grew into long-term commitment, rather than using them to fuel unhealthy ones.

Those who have suffered as I have only need first to have an awakening that something is wrong (which you have had if you are reading this book), educate themselves on the dynamics of toxic attraction (which you will when you read this book), and take preventative and defensive action in the future against tolerating abuse, which I know you are strong enough to do.

Those unaware of what is causing their unhealthy relationship history are doomed to repeat it, and the longer they wait to examine what is going on, the longer the toxic dynamic solidifies in their minds.

Do not let the cycle continue. There is a whole world out there with a potential partner who will appreciate you, benefit from your gifts, and reciprocate your affection instead of asking you to change for them, causing you to doubt yourself, and draining your energy completely. Enhance your understanding and begin the healing process today; it is my hope that you will enjoy and benefit from this book!

Chapter 1: 15 Warning Signs of a Toxic Relationship

ONE OF THE FIRST–AND sometimes hardest–steps of getting out and healing from a toxic relationship is realizing you are a part of one. As an empath, the realization can become harder because we feel deeper than other people. Therefore, the same questions everyone has of "How did this happen?" "Why did I let myself get trapped?" "Why didn't I notice the signs earlier?" tear at us a bit deeper. There is nothing wrong with us when this happens as it is all part of our gift. Yes, I know sometimes our empathic abilities seem more like a curse, but they aren't. They are a wonderful gift we received from the universe, which allows us to try to help people in a way someone else can't. Unfortunately, this can also connect us to some personalities, such as narcissism, which can become toxic.

As you read the warning signs, there is one factor you need to keep in mind: every relationship and every person is different. In reality, there are well over 40 warning signs of a toxic relationship. Just because you don't have one or two warning signs doesn't mean you aren't in a toxic relationship. I understand how it is easy to say, "That doesn't fit my relationship, so it's not toxic." The truth is, that warning sign might not be a part of your relationship, or you haven't noticed it yet. Either way, it is important you understand these warnings signs.

It's also important to know that these warning signs can be hard to see. At the beginning of a relationship, we are in a cloud-nine phase. We believe the person we are with is our soul mate. We love them, and we think they would never hurt us.

We strive to make them happy as we imagine building a family, buying our dream home, and growing old with this person. Love can cloud our judgment and even blind us from seeing the truth.

Sometimes you might feel something isn't right. Empaths often have gut feelings that we don't always understand. If you ever receive one of these gut feelings that something isn't right, you just can't put your finger on it–take note of the feeling. What are your thoughts? What are your emotions? Listen to your instincts as they will help you notice some of these early warning signs.

1. Let's Talk About Me

ONE OF THE WELL-KNOWN personality traits of a narcissist is their ability to talk about themselves. While everyone feels the world revolves around them a little, narcissists will take this belief to the extreme as they genuinely feel the world does revolve around them.

You are sitting down for a nice dinner at your favorite restaurant with the significant other you've been dating for three months. You smile and say, "I love this place. I've come here since I was a little girl. My mom..." Then, they interrupt you by saying, "I've never been here before; it's not really my style. But I will do anything to make you happy because I love you." Your partner then looks back to the menu, so you continue your story. A few seconds into it, they begin to talk about themselves again.

It's important to realize that he isn't like your friend who often talks about themselves. A narcissist is a person who is uninteresting in hearing about anyone else's life. Because they have no sense of morals, they won't even try to look or sound interested in your life. They won't ask you questions to get to know you better because they don't care. They aren't in the relationship to get to know you. They are in the relationship so you can help them. You can give them what they want. You will listen as they talk about themselves. You will be their cheerleader and give them sympathy when they want it. For example, they will never ask you how your day went. You want to find someone who will look at you and ask, "How did your day go today?" or "How are you feeling today?"

2. They Turn Other People Against You

YOU WILL START TO HEAR phrases like, "They don't care for you" or "My family doesn't like you" early in the relationship. These statements usually come out when you are having an argument or you have done something to make your significant other unsatisfied. If you question why they would say something like that, you might hear them describing your actions or behaviors they want to change. It's important to remember that when your partner says something like this to you, they aren't talking about their family members, friends, or your friends. They are talking about themselves. They are trying to trick you into changing your behavior for them. Everyone wants to be liked and a narcissist understands this. Therefore, this can quickly become one of their manipulative tactics or mind games.

3. They are Manipulative

NARCISSISTS ARE KNOWN as master manipulators. Manipulation is when someone tries to change another person's behavior to get what they want. There are several forms of manipulations. If you notice your significant other talks down to you, such as saying, "Don't be silly" or "Don't be stupid" they are using manipulation. Another example of manipulation is to use their size to tower over you as they threaten you. They will also bully you or create jokes at your expense. I will talk about manipulation in greater detail later in this book. However, I felt it was important to mention here because it is a common warning sign of a narcissist.

4. Fragmented Childhood

PEOPLE AREN'T BORN with narcissistic tendencies; they are created in a person who had a difficult childhood. Usually, a narcissist's childhood holds stories of abuse and neglect. Narcissists might not talk much about their childhood but when they do, it doesn't make sense. While they might paint a picture of a perfect family, you can see the holes in the stories or see the story differently. For example, your date might talk about how amazing their family is, but they never truly give you a reason why. Even when you ask, they tend to dance around the answer, change the subject, or act like they didn't hear you. You might also notice they start to get a little more aggressive, especially if you continue asking "why." For instance, their tone might start to become defensive.

5. They Seem Incredibly Charming...Maybe Too Charming

AT FIRST, IT DOES SEEM like our new partner is incredibly charming. In fact, you can believe they are almost perfect. For example, you wake up every morning to a text from your them that says, "Have a great day. I love you." You might also receive the same type of messages throughout your day. They seem to take a keen interest in your life, what you are doing, where you are going, and how you feel. They will give you calls, gifts, and make you feel special.

They make you feel this way because narcissists believe they can only be with someone special. They think that the average person is beneath them and they shouldn't spend their time with them. Another reason is that narcissists believe the only people who can appreciate them is someone on their level (Kassel, 2019).

They will continue to be incredibly charming until you do or say something that they don't like. They won't tell you what you did. They will just start to treat you differently. For example, they won't send you a text right away in the morning. In fact, they might not send you a text at all one day. Questioning them about it will make them react in different ways. They might give you a reason, tell you they were busy, or apologize for their behavior.

6. The World "Love" Comes Out a Little Early

IF YOU HEAR THE PHRASE "I love you" early in the relationship, you want to take note. This is a red flag when it comes to a narcissist. They will create artificial connections in the early stages of a relationship. While you might feel that it is too early in the relationship for the "L" word, your emotions will pull you a different way. Your emotions will start to make a stronger connection to them because you feel like they care. Your mind might not believe what they are saying is true, but your heart is going to tell you something different.

The bottom line is–if you feel that your special someone is saying "I love you" too soon into the relationship, you need to pay attention to this. There might be several reasons why you feel this way. First, it probably is too soon to have such a deep connection. Second, your instincts are trying to get your attention. Third, it's another sign that something isn't right in your relationship.

7. They will Gaslight You

GASLIGHTING IS ONE of the biggest mind games a narcissist uses. When you are gaslighted, you start to question your reality. For example, you'll notice a behavioral change in your partner. They have gone from showing you affection, texting and calling you daily, and giving you gifts to acting distant and cold. You bring it up to them as you want to know if something is wrong or what is going on. They gaslight you by saying, "You're just imagining this. I brought you chocolates not too long ago." After this, they slip back into their affectionate and caring ways. However, several weeks later, you start to notice their cold behaviors creeping back. Of course, when you bring it up again, they tell you the same thing they said last time. This cycle will repeat, causing you to start questioning your reality and mental stability.

Signs of gaslight include:

- You are often apologizing

- Your self-confidence has declined

- You feel more anxious than normal

- You question your sensitivity by wondering if you are overly sensitive

- You don't feel like the person you were before you started dating your significant other

- You feel you can't do anything right

- You feel that something is wrong, but you can't put your finger on what it is

- You blame yourself when something goes wrong, even if it's not your fault

- You create excuses for your significant other's behavior

8. Long-Term Friends Aren't on the List

IF YOU HAVE BEEN DATING for several months and you haven't met their friends, or they rarely talk about their friends, it's time to pay a little more attention. Narcissists have a hard time keeping friends because most people feel they are toxic. While people might hang out with them for a while, they usually start to back away once they begin to notice their challenging personality characteristics.

9. They Never Apologize

YOU FIND YOURSELF APOLOGIZING all the time. You feel that nearly everything that goes wrong is your fault. As you are contemplating your emotions and behaviors, you start to realize that you have changed. You are no longer as confident as you once were. You begin to feel like you are losing your identity. You then think about how often something happens because of your partner. You think about all the times you've had to make up excuses or apologize because of their mistakes or poor behavior. You then come to realize that you have never heard the words "I'm sorry" or "I apologize."

One of the defining factors of a narcissist is that they won't apologize because they haven't done anything wrong. They are always right, and it's everyone else who makes mistakes. If you notice you've never heard the words "I'm sorry" from your significant other, it's time to look at other warning signs of a toxic relationship.

10. You're Walking on Eggshells

WALKING ON EGGSHELLS means you are cautious about everything you say and do because you don't want to make your significant other angry. Narcissists are quick to anger, so it doesn't take you long to realize they have a temper. The biggest problem is, you never truly know what is going to set them off. You can do something one day that you have been doing every day for weeks, and they become angry over it. Their wrath is often frightening for many people and can lead to violence. For example, you are cleaning your home, and you accidentally break a vase. This is a vase that you bought at a garage sale and that didn't hold any special meaning. However, your partner noticing everything that changes and the last time you broke something, which was a glass, they yelled at you like a child. In fact, they told you that you are careless, can't do anything right, and that you're worse than a child. You still remember the words exactly as they were told because they were like a thousand needles stabbing you in the heart. Therefore, you quickly think of what to do. Of course, you need to clean up the mess but you wonder if you should run out and buy a different vase. Maybe he won't notice if you can buy a similar blue vase. As you are cleaning up the shattered pieces, your heart begins to race as you feel a panic attack coming on. You stop to take a few deep breaths as a way to try to calm your nerves.

11. You Are Emotionally Drained

IT'S EASY FOR AN EMPATH to feel emotionally drained. This is why it's important to take some "me time" and recharge. As long as you continue to do this daily, you will recharge and be ready to face another day. Unfortunately, when you are in a toxic relationship, it is hard to recharge. This doesn't happen because you can't find the "me time" to do it–it happens because your significant other is full of negativity. This means that your home, car, any place they have been is filled with their energy. This can cause you to become depressed, which can lead to other psychological problems. If you feel that you are no longer recharging like you used to, it's time to take an in-depth look into your relationship.

12. You Need to Follow Strict Roles

NARCISSISTS NEED TO be in control. They will start to take control early in the relationship. This usually happens gradually, so you won't notice it right away. While you will eventually notice a gradual change, it is hard to catch it as it starts to happen. One factor about your new role is you feel the need to keep it. You know that what you are doing works as it makes your significant other happy. Therefore, even if you aren't happy, you are going to follow through as you don't want to make them angry. This is one of the ways that narcissists trap you in the relationship.

13. They Break You Down

NO MATTER HOW LONG you have been together, your partner knows how to make you feel bad, push your buttons, and break you down. They know how to make you feel certain emotions, which they will use to benefit themselves. For instance, you are having an argument with your partner. You have brought up behaviors that are a red flag for narcissism and telling your partner you will no longer tolerate certain behaviors. As a way to turn the attention away from the behavior that the narcissist wants to hide or deny, they start to blame you. They tell you the only reason they control you is because you act like a child and you need them to help you grow. They then tell you that you can't reach your dreams and goals without them. They will do this so often that you will start to believe them.

14. They Lie

AS AN EMPATH, IT IS easy to tell when someone is lying. We get this gut feeling that something isn't right and sometimes we think, "That's not true." The problem is because so many of us struggle with our instincts, thoughts, and feelings that we don't want to act on them. We think to ourselves, "What happens if my feelings are wrong?" We think about how much we would hurt the other person and damage our relationship. These are thoughts that we cannot handle to come true. Therefore, we find it easier to stay quiet, often causing ourselves to suffer in silence.

If you are conversing with your significant other and they say something that makes you believe they are lying, believe in yourself. It will take a lot of courage to call them out on a lie, but you will feel better. On top of this, you will start standing up for yourself and take back some control.

15. You Give More than You Get

EMPATHS ARE GIVERS, and we don't mind going above and beyond for other people. While many relationships will have one person who gives more than takes, it is usually pretty equal or it works for the couple. However, when an empath and narcissist are together, the empath gives and the narcissist takes. Even when they are doing something, such as giving you chocolates and flowers, they have a motive. Everything a narcissist does is always for themselves. They aren't capable of giving like most people because their brains aren't wired that way.

Chapter 2: What Is a Narcissist and How Do I Attract Them?

YOU OFTEN HEAR AND say the word "narcissist," but do you really know what the word means? Because it is a psychological personality disorder, there are clinical definitions that professional psychologists and therapists need to follow while they are diagnosing their patients.

It's important to realize that narcissism is a personality disorder. They don't think and feel the same way an average person does because they aren't wired to do so. There is a debate on how Narcissistic Personality disorder grows in a person, but many experts believe it is due to childhood trauma and genes. However, the study of genes is still in its early stages of development, which means there is a lot more research needed to make this conclusive. No matter how your significant other came to become narcissistic, you need to realize they can't control their behavior without extensive therapy and medication. Of course, it's extremely difficult to get a narcissist to believe they need therapy because, in their mind, they are perfect.

Understanding Narcissistic Personality Disorder is going to help you overcome the effects of your toxic relationship. It will bring you a sense of peace, allowing you to realize several factors that are always on an empath's mind during and after a toxic relationship.

1. It is not your fault.
2. You could not do anything to help them overcome their narcissism.

3. You *can't* fix them.

Common Characteristics of a Narcissist

SOME OF THESE CHARACTERISTICS, such as controlling behavior and gaslighting, I've discussed in the previous chapter. However, there are several common characteristics of a narcissist that deserve to be highlighted.

Grandiose Sense of Self Importance

IN TODAY'S SOCIETY, people often say, "They are narcissistic" when someone talks about themselves highly. Another word used to explain this is arrogant; however, there is a difference between grandiose and arrogant.

When someone is arrogant, they believe they are the best, but won't use their arrogance to hurt someone they love and care about. They still consider how their statements and actions will make other people feel. They also think of their financial future. When someone is grandiose, they don't care who they hurt in order to make themselves feel more important. They also don't think too much of any financial considerations because this doesn't affect them.

A narcissist expects to be recognized as better than everyone else. They also don't believe they need to work for their achievements. People should simply give them what they want because of who they are. They will exaggerate their achievements to give people the impression they are better than anyone else. A narcissist needs people to believe they are special.

A grandiose sense of self-importance is one of the key characteristics of narcissism because it is easy to spot. It's important to note that this is a natural characteristic of a narcissistic person. They can't hide this part of them from anyone. Therefore, it can also be a warning sign of a narcissist. If you are dating someone and they are constantly talking about how great they are and their amazing accomplishments, turn on your detective skills. You want to look for proof of their achievements. If you are dating a narcissist, you will quickly realize that they are exaggerating.

Lacks Empathy

THE VERY CHARACTERISTIC that you are full of, they lack. Most people have empathy within them. Some people will feel it stronger than others. The amount of empathy we have inside of us doesn't mean one person is better than the other. It means that people with more empathy, like you, have a special gift to help understand a person better. This is why it's important for you to understand Narcissistic Personality Disorder.

Empathy is when a person can feel someone else's emotions. They are absorbed into you. You don't need to talk to the person; you can feel when someone is sad, mad, frustrated, excited, happy, or lonely just by walking into a room. Sometimes, you feel the emotion so strongly it becomes overwhelming and feels like it takes your breath away. Narcissists aren't able to understand this because they don't show empathy. Empathy doesn't tell them how they feel, and it's not going to help them get what they want. Therefore, they aren't going to try to develop empathy.

The fact is, everyone is born with empathy. For some of us, it develops strongly naturally. Other people will spend their time enhancing their empathy, so they can do what they can to help people. Narcissists won't care to develop their empathy. If they do start to feel a little empathic, especially in their younger years when narcissism is starting to develop, they will push it off to the side or ignore it. Empathy is a trait inside of us that we need to use to let it grow. When we don't use it, it's going to become stale.

Strong Fantasies

IN A SENSE, NARCISSISTS live in a fantasy world, and you probably know exactly what I am talking about. For example, in your efforts to try to help your narcissistic partner, you tried to get them to see the error of their ways. You gave them examples, and you might have even recorded them so they could watch their own behavior. However, nothing seemed to work. They never seemed to grasp what you were saying. Instead, they would tell you how great they looked.

It doesn't matter what they are fantasizing about, whether it is power, intelligence or love, they need it and they will have it. They will deny everything that points to their poor behavior or doesn't put them in the light they have for themselves. Many people believe that a narcissist denies their actions as a way to ignore how they look to other people. This isn't necessarily true. When a narcissist's fantasy world becomes strong, they truly believe that other people are telling lies about them. They don't see themselves as other people do. They might even start to believe that other people are out to get them.

Believe People are Envious

NARCISSISTS BELIEVE that people want to be just like them. They truly believe they are one of the best, if not the best person in this world. They are more important than some of the most powerful people in the world. Therefore, why would someone not be jealous of them? If you heard your significant other talk about how "They are just jealous" or "They wish they could be as great as I am" they are narcissistic.

Types of Narcissists

ONE FACTOR I DO NOT want you taking away from this book is that narcissists are out to get empaths. Narcissists aren't out to get anyone. No one is out to get you because you are an empath. What a narcissist wants is what you are going to offer them—what you would offer anyone —your compassion, love, forgiveness, and other personality characteristics.

There are different types of narcissists and it's important that you are able to distinguish between these types because each brings different traits and problems to the table.

First, let's start out with the two main types of narcissists:

Invulnerable Narcissists

ALL NARCISSISTS WILL have the typical behavioral patterns that we already discussed, such as the grandiose sense of self and believing people are jealous of them. However, narcissists will also break down into other behavioral patterns, which is how we get the two main types and the various subtypes.

An invulnerable narcissist is the stereotypical narcissist. They are the ones who are extremely self-confident, they don't worry about other people, they use people, they are manipulative, and they only have emotions for themselves. They want recognition and they want people to believe that they are special.

Many psychologists will explain invulnerable narcissist as suffering from the god complex. This is when people truly believe that they have special personality characteristics that make them better than anyone else (Luna, n.d.).

Vulnerable Narcissists

VULNERABLE NARCISSISTS have many of the same characteristics as invulnerable narcissists; however, they are sensitive. They do care about other people's emotions and understand that they can harm people with their behavior. In fact, many people have started to refer to vulnerable narcissists as "empathic narcissists." Whether you want to refer to them as empaths is up to you. The factors you need to remember are the differences between a narcissist, even one who is sensitive, and empaths.

I want to take time to discuss that you should not try to diagnose yourself as an empathic narcissist. Everyone has a tendency to be a little narcissistic. This is because no matter how much we strive to help other people, we do have a little tendency to believe the world revolves around ourselves. We think that our problems are larger than what they really are. Just because you sometimes think "what is best for me?" or "What do I want to gain out of this?" doesn't mean you are narcissistic. It means you are human.

Deep down, vulnerable narcissists see themselves as unworthy. They struggle with self-love because they don't have high self-esteem. While they will act like they are better than everyone else, they are simply trying to mask how they really feel which is that everyone is better than them.

Within the two main types are four subtypes.

The Compensatory Narcissist

THIS TYPE OF NARCISSIST needs to put on a show to people to make themselves manage their past traumas. Because they struggle to handle criticism, they will only focus on people who are emotionally sensitive. They want people they view as emotionally weak as they will be able to assert their control over the person easier. Furthermore, empaths will allow them to tell their fabricated stories, give them sympathy, and make them feel emotionally stronger. Empaths will give the compensatory narcissist the praise they crave. To get what they want, this type of narcissist will focus on manipulation.

The Amorous Narcissist

THE AMOROUS NARCISSIST focuses on their sexual adventures to get what they want. There is only one reason they will spend their time on someone and that is so they can have a sexual relationship and move on. They pride themselves on the number of people they have had sexual encounters with. While they might hold a serious relationship for a period of time, it generally isn't that long. Once they get what they want, they will move on to their next target.

The Malignant Narcissist

THE MALIGNANT NARCISSIST is one of the most dangerous types because they don't care what they are doing or who they hurt in the process. In fact, some will find delight in hurting other people. They will often be found in prisons and gangs as they typically use violence and break laws to get what they want. They don't have any type of moral value in their life as they don't see the point. They are often referred to as psychopaths, but they can also find the antisocial personality disorder spectrum.

The Elitist Narcissist

WHEN YOU THINK OF A narcissist who has an enormous ego, you are thinking of the elitist. They believe that they are special and unique. They are better than other people and everyone should know this naturally; meaning, they shouldn't have to tell people. They believe that just by seeing them, you know that they are the best person you have ever met. It doesn't matter if you are the narcissist's family member, partner or coworker, they have a sense of entitlement in all areas of their life. They will often brag about themselves and believe that everyone should praise them.

Why Me?

YOU PROBABLY ASKED yourself the "why me?" question several times throughout your toxic relationship. In fact, you probably still ask yourself this question. The truth is, there is this invisible magnet that connects empaths and narcissists. Both types of people are able to sense the other's personality traits unconsciously. For an empath, we see someone who is emotionally and mentally harmed. For a narcissist, they see someone who they can easily control and take advantage of. They see someone who is going to give them what they want.

Opposites Attract

IF YOU HAVE EVER HEARD the phrase "opposites attract," it's true when it comes to narcissists and empaths. When we look for a partner, we look for someone who is going to help balance us. Because empaths struggle to focus on themselves, they are going to find someone who knows how to focus on themselves. Learning how to focus more on ourselves will help balance us as it will allow us to realize when we are putting in too much effort and not getting enough back in return. Furthermore, it will help us recharge, so we can continue to use our empathic abilities to help other people. Think of it this way–learning to take the "me time" we need will help our minds, emotions, and life become more peaceful. This will allow us to think more clearly, which will help us strengthen our abilities to help others.

Opposites attracting bring us back to the give and take role between empaths and a narcissist. You give to a narcissist because you want to help them. You want them to heal from their internal wounds that most people cannot feel. These are wounds that you feel so strongly, and it pains you to feel them. This brings you to understand them a little more. At this point, it is often so early in the relationship that you don't realize their narcissistic tendencies. As you continue to give, they continue to take as this helps them feel more powerful. It feeds their narcissistic characteristics.

Narcissists are Wounded

WE CAN FEEL THE WOUNDS a narcissist has more than they can. We can sense their emotional and psychological hurt and pain. Because we run on our emotions, this overwhelms us, and we want to do whatever we can to help them heal.

When you meet a narcissist, you can feel their pain. You then see how they are trying to get the approval that people so desperately want. It doesn't matter if you are a narcissist, an empath, or anyone else; we all have a basic human need to feel love and approval. You believe you can help them reach this approval and this will make their life so much better. Empaths are healers, and we want to do whatever we can to heal someone's emotional wounds.

Unfortunately, narcissists aren't going to see an empath as a way to help them emotionally heal. They are going to see you as someone who can give them the validation they crave. They don't think that they need to change, the narcissist is thinking about how much attention and praise you will give them.

Empaths Ignore Negative Behavior

WHILE YOU MIGHT NOTICE negative behavior or emotions, you are going to push them to the side. We do this because it helps us to focus more on the positive. As we absorb emotions, they can become overwhelming, causing us to suffer. As healers, we know we can't help someone if we are suffering internally. Therefore, we decide to do what we can to block out any negativity. The problem is, these emotions are still attached to us until we take the time to cleanse ourselves.

Empaths Become Blind to Harmful Behavior

WE KNOW WHEN SOMEONE is emotionally, physically, or psychologically harming us. However, we often take the "they are healing" or the "they can't help it" approach as a way to understand their behavior. When you start to think this way, you open the door for them to continue the behavior. You allow yourself to be an emotional punching bag as you believe this will help them heal. Over time, you become used to the behavior that it blinds you. This means you don't even realize it is happening. Unfortunately, all this does is allow the behavior and relationship to continue. It also drags you deeper into the toxic relationship. The deeper you get into the relationship, the harder it is to get out and the more you have to take time to heal from the effects.

Empaths want to do what they can to heal the world. This is because we can help people heal through our gifts. We help people feel like they are not alone, and we understand what they are feeling. This automatically starts to help people heal because we want other people to understand. It gives people a strong sense of support that they are often lacking during difficult moments. Even though it can get us trapped in a toxic relationship, it is also an amazing gift.

At the same time, we feel emotions stronger and this includes our own. I understand the feeling you can have when you read the above information. You feel that your part of the reason you became trapped in a toxic relationship. In reality, what traps you such a relationship is not understanding the magnetic connection empathy and narcissists have. Another reason is not understanding narcissism. The more knowledge you gain about narcissists and yourself, the more you will be able to protect yourself from another toxic relationship. Furthermore, you will be able to find the courage to leave a toxic relations and heal.

Chapter 3: Toxic Puzzle Pieces: Complementary Characteristics of Empath and Narcissist

WHEN TWO PEOPLE GET together, they connect and complete a puzzle. Even though a relationship between an empath and narcissist becomes toxic, they still complement each other and create a puzzle.

Because I have discussed the characteristics of a Narcissist, I want to take some time to discuss common characteristics of an empath. While most of you already understand the basics, it's important that you have a good understanding of both so you can get a better grasp of how the toxic puzzle pieces together.

Characteristics of an Empath

You Know

IT'S HARD TO EXPLAIN why you know. It's just a gut feeling or a thought that pops into your mind. What you know depends on how attuned you are to your empathic abilities. For instance, you might know that whatever situation has popped up in your life, it's going to be all right. You have a feeling that there will be a couple more bumps along the path, but everything will be just fine in the end. You might wake up one morning and think that something big is going to happen. You don't know exactly what, but you realize what you knew when you receive a call from your friend that they just got engaged. You also know when something doesn't feel right. For instance, when you meet someone and start talking. While they seem nice, you have this feeling that something isn't right about them. You might have felt this way when you first met your current or previous partner.

Like most people, empaths struggle to understand why they know certain factors, which makes them remain quiet about everything. You don't say anything because you are afraid of being wrong and hurting someone's feelings. You don't say anything because you don't fully trust your instincts. You don't say anything because you want your feeling or thought to be wrong. No matter how much you try to remain quiet or push these thoughts and feelings to the side, the bottom line is–you do know.

You're Easily Overwhelmed

WHILE I'VE ALREADY mentioned emotions can make you feel overwhelmed, there are many other factors. For example, public places can become overwhelming. You don't have to meet or talk to people to absorb their emotions. This can make going to supermarkets, concerts, school performances, and even the post office overwhelming. You can walk by a group on the sidewalk and feel overwhelmed by their emotions.

When emotions become too overwhelming, you start to feel like you are suffocating. The emotions are coming from all directions, and it starts to seem like your head is spinning as you try to maintain control. When you get to this point, it's hard to separate the emotions you are feeling. You not only struggle with your negative and positive emotions but also with what emotions are yours and which ones you are absorbing.

You Can't Tolerate Any Type of Violence

AS AN EMPATH, YOU FIND yourself struggling to watch violence on television. This doesn't just include movies, but also television shows and the news. In fact, you might stop watching the news because you can't tolerate hearing about the murders, how many people are fighting, and other types of negative news. This doesn't just include what you see on television but also what you read. You don't read novels that could have violence, news headlines, or anything else.

The stronger your empathic abilities are, the worse it's going to make you feel. Many empaths completely stop listening or reading current events as they can't tolerate the way the world is going. However, it's always a good idea to pay attention to positive news headlines. For example, read the headlines about someone building a new homeless shelter in your area of giving back to the community in other ways. Focusing on the positives can help you control your negative emotions and make it easier for you to cleanse when you take your "me time."

You Are a Continuous Counselor

IT DOESN'T MATTER WHERE you are or who you are with when you see someone who needs help, you are going to help them. In fact, you are like a magnet to people who need someone to talk to. There is something about the aura of empaths that makes people feel they can talk to you. Furthermore, people feel comfortable around you, which makes them feel they can open up and not be judged. While you might question why this happens from time to time, this is part of your great gift, and you should be proud of it. There aren't a lot of people in this world who are empaths, which makes our emotional powers even more unique and special.

Yes, I understand, it can be overwhelming to have people come to you about their problems. In fact, it can often become uncomfortable. As long as you are always safe and you can take care of yourself, allow yourself to spread your gift into the world.

You Forget About Self-Care

SELF-CARE IS IMPORTANT for everyone, but it is more important for an empath. You need to take time every day, sometimes more than once, to cleanse your emotions and connect yourself to the universe. Doing this will give you peace of mind and help you become emotionally balanced. There are a lot of ways you can cleanse your emotions. For example, you can walk barefoot in the grass, meditate, find time to be alone and do something you enjoy, or lay in the sun, close your eyes, and enjoy the peace. Whatever you do, you need to focus on you.

If you continue to help people and absorb emotions without taking time for yourself, you're going to find yourself exhausted. You will lack energy, struggle to complete daily tasks, become moody, and find yourself becoming overly frustrated with other people.

Complementary Characteristics

NOW THAT YOU HAVE CHARACTERISTICS for a narcissist and empath, we can start piecing together the puzzle to why narcissists and empaths complement each other. When couple complement each other, they each bring something into the relationship. For example, one person might cook while the other person cleans. Unfortunately, when an empath gets together with a narcissist, there isn't a balance between give and take. Instead, narcissists take what the empaths give.

Empaths are the Important Ones

WHEN A NARCISSIST IS looking for a partner, there are many features they are going to look for. First, they need someone they believe is special. Second, they need someone who is going to make them believe they are important. At the same time, they are also looking for someone who is going to see them as important. Empaths are the perfect person to fill these needs for a narcissist.

Empaths are Patient and a Narcissist Needs Patience

THERE ARE MANY PARTS of life we need to have patience. It doesn't matter if you are an empath or a narcissist, you will run into areas in your life where patience is needed. When narcissists lose their patience, their anger takes over. This isn't good for them because a narcissist thrives on what others feel and believe about them. If they allow their anger to take over, people are going to see them as an angry person. People will then become less likely to see them in an uplifting light. Instead of seeing them as an important person, they will see them as cold and heartless. Therefore, to gain patience, a narcissist turns to an empath.

Empaths Give Off Positive Energy, Which a Narcissist Takes

NARCISSISTS FEED OFF of an empath's positive energy. No matter what a person is going through or what type of psychological disorder they have, people need positive energy. It's a human need that absolutely everyone needs to feel. The problem for a narcissist is they don't often feel positive energy; they only feel negative energy. This is one of the biggest reasons why a narcissist becomes attached to an empath. They are able to absorb the positive energy that an empath holds and tries to keep in their environment.

The biggest problem with this is, there can only be so much energy in a person or a room. Therefore, when your positive energy is taken from a narcissist and replaced with their negative energy, you don't have enough room for more positive energy. To bring positive energy back into your life, you need to cleanse yourself and your environment. Wherever the narcissist has been, you need to take time to clear the negative energy and allow the positive energy to return.

If you don't take your time to cleanse, you are going to fill your environment with a large amount of negative energy. This is damaging to anyone but can be especially damaging to an empath because you feel emotions at a higher level. Negative energies cause people to become frustrated, angry, and depressed. You can find yourself emotionally dragging for more than one reason. The longer you let this go on, the worse it will be.

Empaths are Highly Sensitive, and a Narcissist Needs Sensitivity

THIS KIND OF FOLLOWS the same path as patience, except it is a little more important. Narcissist don't care about other people. At the same time, narcissists depend on people believing they are a good person. Take a moment to ask yourself–would you believe someone is a good person if they didn't show any type of sensitivity? You saw them as cold-hearted and self-absorbed. Okay, you are an empath, so, yes, you will still believe there is some good in the person. But, people who do not have empathic abilities will not believe there is any type of good in that person.

A narcissist can't get people to believe they are a great person if they don't show sensitivity. Not only will a narcissist be able to feed off the sensitivity, as they do to an empath's emotions, but they will be able to learn how to act in a sensitive way. A narcissist is always paying attention to their surroundings because they have to defend themselves. They are very alert, which means they pay attention when their partner is showering people with sensitivity. They will pick up on your tone of voice, how you act, and how you treat people. They will then use what they learn to manipulate people into believing they are a sensitive person. This will make people see a narcissist as special, which is exactly what a narcissist wants.

Empaths Fear Abandonment While a Narcissist Fears Commitment

SOME OF THE EMPATH'S biggest fears are loss, rejection, and abandonment. On the other side of the coin, a narcissist fears commitment and vulnerability. Fears are some of our strongest emotions, and we look toward other people to help us with our fears.

An empath's fear of abandonment is comforted through a narcissist because they need an empath. They take what an empath has to give. Therefore, even if the relationship is unhealthy, a narcissist is never going to leave an empath. This doesn't mean that they will remain faithful. It simply means they will continue to use you as long as you stay with them.

One of the strongest traits an empath will give someone is commitment, which is what the narcissist fears. However, the narcissist is also able to control the relationship, which limits their fears. Furthermore, a narcissist doesn't see their relationship with an empath as a form of commitment. They are using the empath for their personal gain. This is completely different than being a relationship where you feel committed to the person. Basically, a narcissist gets what they need without having to take the step to true commitment, at least in their mind.

Empaths Have Forgiving Hearts, and a Narcissist Is Defensive

EMPATHS ARE QUICK TO forgive. In fact, you probably notice you don't stay angry at someone long. You understand that people make mistakes and believe they are doing their best. This helps you find room to forgive people easily. Furthermore, an empath's gift doesn't allow them to stay angry for too long, as long as they are cleansing. Holding grudges keeps the negative emotions inside of us. When we take time to cleanse and have alone time, we are letting the negativity and harm people have done to us. This allows you to have a forgiving heart.

A forgiving heart works well with a narcissist who is going to deny and defend their actions and behaviors. It doesn't matter what they do or how much they hurt you mentally, emotionally or physically, they will defend themselves. This means you can choose to stay angry with them or you can choose to forgive them. Most of the time, an empath's choice is to forgive. This helps a narcissist as it allows them to continue their behavior without you holding their past against them.

Empaths Lift People's Spirits, and a Narcissist Needs to Feel Important

A NARCISSIST BELIEVES they are a highly important person. But this doesn't mean they don't need other people to feel the same way. In fact, one of the biggest reasons a narcissist thinks so highly of themselves is because they find people who make them feel important, such as an empath.

Empaths want people to feel special because this makes people feel happy. It makes people feel like they matter. They will strive to make anyone feel this way; however, they will focus more on the people they are attached to, such as their significant other. A narcissist will often use manipulation to get an empath to make them feel important. For example, they might say that they acted a certain way because they aren't happy with themselves. They might say they said something because they don't feel like you see them as special. As empaths, hearing the person we love and care about say this breaks our heart. Therefore, we will go out of our way to make our significant other feel better.

Chapter 4: Empath to the Rescue! Why Do Women Often Want to "Fix" Men Showing Wounded Behavior?

I WANT TO TAKE THE time to mention that empaths can be male or female just as narcissists can be either gender. However, for the purpose of this book, I am focusing on how empathic women want to "fix" narcissist men.

Additionally, if you would like to explore your own personal empathy further, please refer to my companion book titled, "Empath Awakening," about empaths and how to stop absorbing negative feelings from others.

How many times have you looked at someone and thought, "I can make them feel better" or started to feel bad for the person? You might get a sense that they are sad, seen them get hurt, or hear a story they told about their abusive childhood. Because you feel a strong connection to someone else's emotions, you are quick to have compassion, understanding, and sympathy. You want to do what you can to make the world a better place for everyone because you want people to feel happy.

You are shopping for groceries when you run into a man in the next aisle. You apologize by telling them that you aren't the best driver. As you see him smile and respond, you get a feeling in the pit of your stomach. You have had this feeling before and you know it's not a pleasant one. You look at the man as he nods "okay" to you and proceeds. You continue to walk into the aisle to pick up your favorite soup, but you can't stop thinking about the feeling the man gave you. As you think more about him, you start to remember his eyes. They look so sad to you. You start to remember how he forced a smile and nodded. You have run into many people in the grocery store before and none of them have ever reacted in such a way.

As you are heading to the checkout lines, you notice that man. You decide to join him in the checkout line. The closer you walk toward him, the stronger the feeling in your stomach becomes and you start to feel his sadness. At the same time, you are overwhelmed by many other negative emotions. Of course, being in a grocery store, you contribute it to the number of people around you. It can't all be from this one person. After all, no one can have that much negative energy around them.

"I just want to apologize again" you say honestly as you are trying to start a conversation. "I really didn't mean to run into your cart back there." At first, you notice the man looks irritated and you immediately begin to question your actions. You didn't mean to make him feel worse or cause any more problems. Suddenly, he turns to you, smiles, and says "It's really no problem. Not everyone can be a great driver like me." You chuckle as you start to question if that was a joke or if he was really giving himself a compliment.

A few days later, you meet your friend at the coffee shop. As you are sitting there talking, you notice a familiar face walks in the door. You think about where you have seen this man before. As your memory of the grocery store encounter comes back to you, you wave at him. He waves back, grabs a coffee, and asks if he could take a seat. You and your friend agree and you all start talking. It doesn't take long for you to notice that while he talks about himself often, something still seems off. The feeling in your stomach and back, so you do your best to watch his facial expressions and gestures more than his words. Before you get up and leave, he asks if he could have your number. You've noticed an attraction to him, so while hesitant, you give him your number. While you don't think he will text or call, you still hold out hope that he does.

A couple of weeks later, he finally calls and asks you out on a date. You agree and meet him at his favorite restaurant. As you meet, he continues to tell you how he can't wait for you to try some of his favorite food. During your conversation, you start to notice that he has emotional wounds. While you can't understand directly where they come from, you can feel it and sense it in his voice. You start to feel they might stem from his childhood as he won't discuss his family or childhood.

At the end of the night, he asks you for another date. You quickly oblige because you are now on a new mission. You need to know where his emotional pain comes from. As an empath, you strive to do your best to ensure that everyone leads a happy life. The more you get to know him, the more you focus on ways to heal his wounds. You try to talk to him as you notice he enjoys talking about himself. However, you can never truly understand where his wounds are coming from. Therefore, you listen closely to him and every time you notice he is acting negatively, you do whatever you can to lift up his spirits. While you don't know how you are going to accomplish it at this moment, you know there is a way that you will be able to fix his emotional wounds.

This story might sound familiar to you. It's a common theme between a narcissist and an empath. The wounds a narcissist has is typically the main reason narcissists and empaths become an item. Empaths want to heal the wounds of a narcissist. As stated before, this is the biggest driving force that brings these two personalities together.

But why? Why do empathic women feel the need to "fix" narcissistic men? Why do empaths, no matter how many times they find themselves trapped in a toxic relationship, continue to come to the rescue?

You Feel It's Your Mission

THE BOTTOM LINE TO the reason why is because you feel it is your mission. It doesn't matter if you are strongly connected to your empathic abilities or not. You feel that you have a calling to help people. Therefore, you find yourself taking wounded people under your wing.

It's an attachment that you really can't explain. Sometimes you will try. You will dig deep to come up with reasons why. You might tell yourself or someone else you tried to help the narcissist because you felt bad for them. You remember seeing them sitting alone at a table talking to the people at the next table. You could hear his conversation and notice how they were trying to ignore him. This broke your heart as you believe everyone deserves to be heard and respected. Therefore, you decided to make him feel better by asking if you could sit next to him. He agreed and soon you were conversing and learning more about him that you imagined. This only strengthened your mission as your emotions became stronger. You could sense his inner pain and you wanted to heal those wounds.

If you understand you are a highly sensitive person and are connected to your empathic gift, you're going to know it's your mission to help. You feel that as long as you take care of yourself, you will be able to keep the positivity in your life going while erasing the negativity from his. However, it doesn't always work this way. Narcissists are just as powerful as empaths with their abilities. They can quickly make you feel overwhelmed and unable to care for yourself.

You Can't Stand to See Anyone Hurting

IT'S JUST HARD TO SEE people hurting. It doesn't matter if they are hurting physically, emotionally or psychologically, you want to do whatever you can to ease their pain. For empaths, seeing a person hurting is similar to watching and hearing about violence. We can't tolerate it well and we want to do whatever we can to end the pain and suffering.

You Are Full of Love

EMPATHS ARE FULL OF love, and they believe they should spread it around. You believe that love can conquer anything, including deep emotional wounds. While you understand it will take time, you are patient. You even understand that the person might become frustrated or angry, but you are forgiving. Because of your love, you feel that you can handle anything that comes your way as you are trying to heal someone.

Love is a positive emotion, but it is also very powerful. When we are full of love, we can forget about the reality of the situation. Love is blinding and this can cause us to fall into a toxic relationship.

You Believe in Them

NO MATTER WHAT A PERSON does or say, they have potential. You believe that everyone has good in them and can work to become a better person. Moreover, you also believe that you can help them become that better person.

The belief in a person become stronger when they are your significant other. Through believing in them, you feel that they can overcome any obstacle that gets in their way. Through your support, you feel that they can accomplish any task they set their mind to. You also feel that it is this support that is going to help heal their wounds.

You Are Nurturing

EMPATHS HAVE A STRONG and natural nurturing instinct. They believe that with some tender loving care, wounds can heal. After all, you are able to heal your own wounds as long as you take time to take care of yourself, right? Why can't you help other people heal the same way?

The truth is, for some people it is too late to give them the nurturing instinct. For example, you meet a narcissistic man who rarely talks about his mother. As you get to learn a little more about his childhood, you realize that his mother abused and neglected him. One of your friends went to school with him and told you how his mother never came to his basketball games because she was too busy with her boyfriend or taking care of herself. You also learn that his mother would bully him. She would also demand that he do whatever she wanted—even if it was illegal. She believed the world revolved around her and everyone should do whatever they could for her.

After you hear this background, your nurturing instinct kicks into overdrive. You realize that he missed an important piece of his childhood because his mother couldn't put her own needs and wants aside for her son. Therefore, you start to think that you can heal his wounds by nurturing him. After all, if we are missing something as powerful as love and acceptance from our mother, we are going to crave it and try to find these factors in other people. As an empath, you decide that you are the best person for this because your heart is full of love and acceptance.

You Believe You Are Their Life Savor

TO AN EMPATH, A NARCISSIST is a mystery. They are someone that is hurting in a way that you can't directly put your finger on. You know that you need to find out the reason for their pain to help them, and you are going to do this because you can save them. After all, what is the point of having your empathic abilities if you can't fix a person?

The truth is, your empathic abilities have nothing to do with fixing a person. What your gift does is allow you to help them overcome their challenges with compassion, love, care, and understanding. You can't help a person unless they want help, and when it comes to a narcissist, getting them to accept help is a large process.

No matter how hard you try to help a narcissist, you are never going to accomplish this task. This isn't because you don't have the empathic abilities you thought you did. It doesn't have anything to do with you. It has everything to do with them. Think of it this way–an alcoholic will not be able to overcome their disease without wanting to change. It's the same way for a narcissist. They have to want to change in order to accept help. They need to change on their own. Of course, if they do decide to go to therapy and find ways to control their narcissistic behavior, you can be supportive. But they need to take the steps on their own.

By now, you might be asking where all this information leaves you. Should you help someone who is wounded? The short answer to this is, you are going to want to help them. Because of your gift, there is nothing you can do to stop the need to help people. At the same time, the last step you want to take is ignoring your willingness to help people. This is an admirable trait, and you should never be ashamed of it. In fact, you should walk around know you are an empath with pride just like an artist has pride in their gift. So, no, you should never ignore any of your empathic abilities. What you need to do is realize you can't be everyone's superwoman. You can't fix anyone. You can only support them as they are trying to change themselves.

Chapter 5: Stages of a Toxic Relationship - Do You Relate?

IT'S IMPORTANT TO ALWAYS remember each relationship is unique. While there are general stages of a toxic relationship, they might not all fit into your relationship. If you only relate to a few of these or half of them, this doesn't mean you aren't in a toxic relationship. The factor you always want to keep in mind is that if you feel you're in a toxic relationship, you need to take care of yourself. Your instinct is always going to tell you more about your relationship than you realize. While you might be cautious about trusting your instinct, it's important to do what you can to try.

Stage One: The Attraction

THE FIRST STAGE OF a toxic relationship is the first of any relationship—the attraction. You are the one who is most likely to become attracted because you are the empath. A narcissist isn't going to become attracted to you at first, unless they are able to sense or see your empathic abilities. For instance, they might see you trying to help someone through a problem with compassion and sympathy, which is what draws them to you. Because of your deep love, you become infatuated with the narcissist every time they are near you. This makes your bond stronger; however, the narcissist will never develop a strong bond with you. They will use you until you leave the relationship or they tell you to leave.

Amirah and David: The Beginning

AMIRAH WAS AN EMPATH learning how to blossom in her abilities. As a 22-year-old, she was fresh out of college and looking for the job of her dreams. She learned about her empathic gift as a college student when she met a friend named Lisa. Through Lisa, Amirah was able to learn how to help people, how to find her inner peace through recharging, and how to make the best out of her gift.

It was only a couple of weeks ago that Amirah left her boyfriend of four years. They went from talking about getting married to going their separate ways when he got a job overseas. She couldn't bear to make that move. While the breakup was tough, they remained friends.

Today, Amirah will admit that she was lonely when she met David at a mutual friend's party. He was standing in the middle of the living room talking about what a great businessman he will make. David was 24-year-old and had been working under her boss, Steve at an automotive parts store. He was on his way to starting his own business.

At first, Amirah didn't think much about David. However, once she started to notice people would walk away from him as he was talking, she started to feel bad for him. She then decided to listen as she didn't want to see him feel bad about himself. After a couple of hours talking, Amirah started to feel that she could help David achieve his dreams. She noticed an internal sadness within David that made her heart break. It was as if he was putting on this mask that wouldn't show his true feelings. She decided one of the best ways she could help David reach his dreams was by being his cheerleader and healing his wounds.

Stage Two: The First Red Flag

IT REALLY DOESN'T TAKE long for a narcissist to show the first red flags. The trick is, the empath needs to understand the signs and pay attention. They also need to be able to overcome denial, listen to their instincts, and believe in what they are noticing. This is often difficult for an empath, at least in the first few months because the narcissist is the center of their attention. They believe they have met their soulmate and they are completely in love. Unfortunately, the narcissist is not in love with the empath. It's hard for narcissists to love anyone because they don't really love themselves truly. We can't love other people in a healthy way without loving ourselves first.

The narcissist will start showing parts of their personality that will make the empath give them all the attention and sympathy they desire. They might become a complainer and tell you that nothing is going right in their life. They don't understand why people treat them horribly as they have done nothing to deserve it. As a healer, you will do whatever you can to try to make them feel better. Unfortunately, you will never be able to help them heal because they do not want the help—they want attention.

Stage Three: Relationship Focuses on the Narcissist

AT THIS POINT, THE empath's intention is still full of love and compassion. They want what is best for the narcissist and continue to try to help their wounds heal. However, they might also start to notice some of the signs, especially if they are aware of these signs. For example, they start to realize that the narcissist doesn't take too much interest in their life. While they try to talk to the narcissist about their problems, the empath is ignored, pushed to the side, or the conversation focuses on the narcissist. This is when the empath starts to feel drained as their emotional and psychological needs are not being met.

This is also the stage where the empath might bring up the problems to the narcissist, which will end up fighting. This can make the empath become afraid to talk to the narcissist about certain issues within their relationship. It is also around this time where the narcissist will start to degrade the empath, whose self-esteem begins to break down.

Amirah and David: A Changing Story

TWO MONTHS INTO THEIR relationship, Amirah started to become a little bored with how often David talked about himself. She also noticed that he would often speak highly about himself. It didn't always make sense or did he always tell the truth. While these mental notes were made in Amirah's mind, she continued to support David as he talked about starting his own business. Sometimes, she would become excited about the adventure. She would think about how successful the business would be and how she could help him in the office. She even imagined how they could go to work together and raise a family while creating their own work schedules.

"I don't know about him" Lisa started to tell her friend. "Something just seems off. It's like he doesn't truly care about you or your dreams. You never wanted to work in an automotive store before."

"Things are different now" Amirah said quietly. "David and I are a couple, and I am starting to fall in love with him.

Seeing him succeed is more important than my dream job. I can always get to my dream job later in my life. David is ready to make the move now. As his partner, it's my job to help him."

"Just be careful" Lisa told her friend. "I think he is hiding something and I don't want to see you hurt."

After her conversation with Lisa, Amirah went to David and told him, "Lisa is such a great friend. I really hope you decide to hang out with us again."

"I won't" David snapped at Amirah. "What I mean is that I tried to get along with Lisa before, remember? We did meet and it didn't go well. She never gave me a chance. You would think if you really loved me you would worry more about how I feel than what Lisa says."

Amirah looked at David a little confused. She didn't get that impression from Lisa. She felt that her friend tried to get to know David, but he kept interrupting her by talking about himself.

"Well, don't you love me anymore?" David asked his girlfriend after a few minutes of silence.

"Of course, I do…I just…" Amirah stated to say, but David quickly left the room, telling her that he had some business to take care of.

Stage Four: The Narcissist Has Control

BY NOW, THE NARCISSIST has almost full control of the empath and their emotions. Even though the empath might feel exhausted and unhappy in the relationship, they will continue to help the narcissist. Part of this is because of control. The narcissist has been able to put the empath up against a wall, which gives them the power. Another part of this is because the empath still feels a sense of responsibility in the relationship. They want to do want they can to continue to heal the narcissist's wounds as they still believe healing is possible. Plus, an empath will feel if they can heal the narcissist, they will be able to heal the relationship.

However, it is also possible that the empath is still in denial about the signs or doesn't understand their partner is a narcissist. They also might be following the love is blind path and not able to see what the narcissist is doing to them, even though they don't feel right. This can also happen when an empath is unaware of their gift. They might think that they are taking on too much or not getting enough sleep.

Amirah and David: Control and Manipulation

"HOW CAN YOU STILL BE talking to her?" David yelled at Amirah, making her jump in the chair. "I thought you loved me and I told her, if you did, you wouldn't let Lisa come between us anymore!"

"I'm not" Amirah said quietly and then waited to see David's expression. She quickly wondered what he was going to do. They had been together six months and within the last couple months, David had started to show a side that Amirah didn't notice before. It was a side that often frightened her into doing what he asked.

"But you are" David replied in a calmer voice. "You are letting her come between us. If you didn't you wouldn't be talking to her anymore. Don't you see what she is doing to me? She is trying to get you to leave me because she has some crazy idea in her mind. You told me that you loved me. You know my mother used to say the same thing and then never prove it to me. You know how much that hurts me. Why are you acting like my mother? I've been so good to you."

"I...I'm sorry" Amirah said as she stood. "I didn't realize I was doing that. I love you. You know I do. I just..."

"There isn't anything else," David said as he backed away. "If you love me, there is nothing else after that. You either stop talking to Lisa or I will leave you. It's her or me."

Stage Five: Empath Reaches a Breaking Point

EMPATHS HAVE A BREAKING point just like everyone else. Eventually, they will have too much of the narcissist's controlling behavior and start to find their voice. Unfortunately, this is also the time when an empath can put themselves in physical danger. Narcissists can become extremely defensive and violent if they feel they aren't getting their way. This can cause them to physically lash out at an empath, which can put more fear into the relationship. The empath and narcissist relationship is already in a damaging cycle, and physical violence is only going to make it worse.

At this point, some empaths might start to go into their protective shell. They will go back to doing what they need to do to keep their partner happy. They feel that as long as they follow the narcissist's ways, they will be able to bring the relationship back to its happy state. At the same time, they can start to feel they are the reason the relationship is breaking. They might think back to the beginning when they were happy and listen to the narcissist when they blame the empath for the problems within their relationship. This is one reason it's important to understand narcissism, your empathic abilities, and how they match together. It will help you realize that you are not at fault and help you take care of yourself as you find your voice.

Other empaths will continue to hold their voice and might start to look for a way out. Unfortunately, there is still a lot of cycling that is going to go on within the relationship. Because the narcissist has come to understand the empath is changing, they will go into damage control mode. There are several ways a narcissist deals with damage control. For instance, they might go back to the caring way there were at the beginning when they were trying to establish control, such as bringing you gifts. They might also want to go to the movies or hang out with you. Other narcissists will focus more on tearing down your self-esteem as they feel this will keep you right where they want you.

The longer the narcissist has control over you, the more frustrated, angry, and tired you will become. The more you will begin to change because the narcissist continues to drain you. This will make it harder for you to work on leaving the relationship. It can also cause you to give up, which is when you will stay in the relationship because you believe there is no way out.

Amirah and David: Amirah's Breaking Point

A YEAR AFTER AMIRAH blocked Lisa from her phone and social media accounts, she was hiding in her home. She worked from home as an artist trying to make enough money to pay the bills. This was a struggle because David refused to help out. He felt his money should go to more important items for himself.

As Amirah was putting the finishing touches on her painting, the lights went out. She quickly looked around the apartment and realized that the city turned off the electricity.

A few minutes later, David came home from work. He tried to turn on the lights. "You're wasting your time," Amirah said quietly. "We don't have electricity."

"How am I going to watch TV?" David snapped at Amirah. "You don't do anything but act like a child painting all day long. Why can't you pay the electric bill?"

"Why can't you help out financially?" Amirah snapped back. While she was always cautious of what she said, Amirah was starting to find her voice in the relationship again. She was getting tired of how David treated her, and she was thinking about leaving the relationship. She just had to figure out how, when, and if she would be able to make it on her own.

"My money is my money. I work hard for every penny I earn, and I shouldn't have to spend any of it to make sure you have lights to act like a child!" David yelled as he grabbed the canvas from Amirah's easel and stomped on it.

"Stop it!" Amirah yelled, "That's for a client! Now I have to start over!"

David looked at Amirah and started laughing. "You stupid little child," he told her. "You seriously think anyone is going to be dumb enough to pay you for something that bad? Who do you think you are?"

Stage Six: Plan to Escape

EVENTUALLY, MOST EMPATHS will start to use this time to think of ways to leave the relationship. This will be easier for some than others. It all depends on several factors, such as how emotionally and mentally strong the empath is. If the narcissist has torn down their self-esteem, they will most likely struggle to leave the relationship. However, if the empath maintains a relatively healthy amount of self-esteem, reaches out for moral support, and is able to stay strong, they will be able to leave the relationship sooner rather than later.

While some will leave quickly, others will focus on leaving at a slower pace. This isn't always because they need to be more cautious and make sure they pick the right time. It can also be because they need to build up their self-worth, so they can be strong when they decide to leave. They realize the stronger they are, the more likely they will stand by their decision and won't find themselves coming back.

Amirah and David: Amirah Finds Her Courage

"I CAN'T DO THIS ANYMORE. You were right," Amirah cried into the phone as she talked to Lisa. "I am so sorry."

"Hey," Lisa replied, "There is nothing you need to be sorry about. Is there anyway you can get away so we can meet up? You can come to my house."

"Tomorrow when David's at work," Amirah replied. "I was actually thinking about packing a bag, but I don't know..."

"Pack a bag and stay with me," Lisa said "You can figure out the rest when you get here. The most important thing is you get out of that house before things get worse."

"I need to go," Amirah whispered into the phone. "I think David's coming and if he sees me on my phone, he will check it. I will call you in the morning."

Stage Seven: Healing

NO MATTER HOW QUICKLY you got out of the toxic relationship, you will need to heal. You will need to maintain a no contact clause where you don't have any type of communication with the narcissist. This is one of the best ways to help yourself heal because you are able to step away from the toxic environment. If you continue to talk to them, you will find yourself drained, which will continue to break you down.

No Contact

UNFORTUNATELY, NO CONTACT is going to be another difficult step in the process. It won't be as simple as blocking their number, blocking them from social media, and never hearing from them again. There will be ways that the narcissist might try to contact you that you never thought about. For example, if they know where you work, they might stop by, send you a gift, or talk to one of your coworkers. If you have mutual friends, they might talk to them and use manipulation and guilt to get them to help get back in contact with you.

However, the narcissist trying to maintain contact might not be a problem at all. The biggest problem with the no-contact clause will be your emotions. In fact, many empaths who have discussed healing after their toxic relationships state that they felt like they were in an emotional prison (Milstead, n.d.). Most of these emotions will be negative and painful, which is why you will struggle to face them. You might even find yourself ignoring them, but you need to do your best to overcome your emotions as this will help you follow your no contact clause.

TOXIC MAGNETISM

Denial is an emotion that will creep up now and then. You might still deny that you were in a toxic relationship at times. Other times you will deny that the narcissist had such negative intentions and drained you of your emotions. You will go back and forth with your denial.

Anger will rear its ugly head in the beginning and can stay with you for a long time. This can cause other problems because empaths struggle more than other people when it comes to having negative emotions. You will be angry at yourself for getting into the relationship and not getting out sooner. You will also be angry with the narcissist for how they treated you. You can find yourself angry at your friends, family members, coworkers, and anyone else you maintained contact with through the relationship.

Anxiety will increase as you worry about what is going to happen. You will worry about if he tries to get back with you and if he doesn't. Sometimes, you will worry that he is lurking around every corner. You might start to become anxious about your mindset as you fear you're losing control of your life. You can start to have panic attacks if the narcissist comes in contact with you or you hear their name. You might also start to have panic attacks as you remember the relationship. This can increase if you find yourself suffering from Post-Traumatic Stress Disorder (PTSD).

You will feel *lonely* and *isolated*. You will feel that no one will be able to understand what you went through. You can even feel that no one will be able to help you get over your toxic relationship. You might find yourself withdrawing from your friends, family, and society as you sink into a depression.

You will feel *ashamed* that you allowed yourself to love a person who could be so heartless. Shame can show itself as you think about how you allow yourself to be treated, why you didn't leave sooner, and how you couldn't help them.

You will go through a stage of *grief* as you let go of the person you loved and cared deeply about. This is similar to the grief you feel when someone dies. While the narcissist is still alive, you need to act like they are dead as you will no longer have contact with them. Your mind and heart will go through the same stage of grief that you do when you suffer a loss.

No matter what you are feeling during your healing and no contact phase, you need to remember that you are not over-emotional. You are healing from a toxic relationship and how you feel is how you feel. You need to acknowledge and accept these emotions as this will be the only way you can really start to heal.

Amirah: The Healing Process

"HOW COULD I ALLOW THIS to happen?" Amirah asked Lisa. "I can't believe I allowed myself to be treated like that for almost two years."

"Hey, that part is over now," Lisa said. "You've been here for a couple of months now and you haven't heard from him since you blocked his number. What you need to focus on now is getting your life back on track. You are still the person you were before you met David. The only difference is you are now stronger and wiser. You will overcome this situation and you will heal from the relationship. You will find your dream job and you will find someone who truly loves you."

"I know," Amirah said as she looked at Lisa and smiled. "It will just take time...lots and lots of time. But I have that job interview on Tuesday. If I get the job, I will be able to build up my resume and work toward getting that dream job I always talked to you about."

"What do you mean if you get it?" Lisa asked. "You will get it. You're smart and an amazing artist. Believe in yourself. You got this."

Chapter 6: Is My Partner An Energy Vampire? Take This Quiz

ENERGY VAMPIRES DO whatever they can to suck all the energy out of you. It's important to know they don't realize they are doing this as it is often at an unconscious level. It is simply who they are.

People often refer to narcissists as energy vampires because of how much energy they take from people, especially an empath. The struggle for many people is understanding and knowing if your partner is an energy vampire. If you answer "yes" to most of these questions, your partner is an energy vampire.

Five Types of Energy Vampires

BEFORE YOU GET INTO the quiz, I want to talk about the four main types of romantic energy vampires.

The Complainer

DO YOU OFTEN GIVE YOUR significant other a solution to their problem and they respond with, "Yes, but..." or "That's not going to work?" The complainer is the energy vampire who will drain you because of the problems they are having. No matter what is going on in their life–everything can seem perfect to you–they are having a problem. Furthermore, they expect you to fix this problem because they don't deserve the issue they are having. It is always someone else's fault and if you can't fix it, it's also your fault. They have the strong "poor me, feel bad for me" attitude and will look for empaths who are extremely sympathetic and willing to comfort this attitude.

The Unintentional Sapper

IT'S IMPORTANT TO NOTE that not all energy vampires realize what they are doing. In fact, some would be devastated to realize they are an energy vampire. This type of energy vampire is known as the unintentional sapper not only because they don't realize what they are doing, but also due to their sensitive nature. They often feel that they have had the worst day and they need to come to you for comfort. However, you struggle to give them the compassion, patience and comfort they need because you are tired.

The Criticizer

NOTHING SEEMS GOOD enough for the criticizer. They will find something wrong with everything you do, even when you feel you have completed the task perfectly. Even if you did something minor, such as forgot to put the newspaper into the recycling bin, they will come to you with their criticism. They will also be incredibly harsh when they criticize. They don't care if they hurt your feelings or not.

The Nagger

WHILE YOU MIGHT FEEL they have your best interest in their heart with their constant reminders, they nag you because they don't believe you are capable of taking care of yourself. They feel they are more responsible than you, which means they have to remind you of everything until you perform the action. They will nag you about anything they feel is important, such as, "Did you take my tux to the cleaner's yet?" or "Did you get a gym membership yet?" The more you slack on the task, the more frustrated and angry they will become. They might even resort to yelling to get you to do what they are telling you to do.

The Self-Obsessor

THIS TYPE OF ENERGY vampire doesn't care at all about your needs. They aren't sensitive, and they feel you should focus on them more than anyone else. They are the most important person in your life. While your partner is always one of the most important people in your life, the self-obsessed will take this to the extreme. They won't care about your emotions, your day, or how you are feeling. They only care about themselves and what they are going through. They will become angry if you don't show interest in what they are telling you. They might even try to make you feel guilty by saying, "You don't love me because you aren't even paying attention to me." When you do try to tell them about how you feel, they will either ignore them, turn to conversation onto them, or downplay your emotions by telling you, "It's not that bad, you're being overdramatic."

Questions:

1. Does Your Partner Often Talk About Themselves?

WHILE MOST PEOPLE TALK about themselves, an energy vampire will talk about themselves more than anyone else. They will interrupt you when you are telling them about your day or even your children. They will interrupt other people's conversations to bring the conversation into their direction. If you feel like your conversations with your partner always turns into what is going on in their lives, what they are thinking, and doing, you are with an energy vampire.

YES or NO

2. Does Your Partner Act Like a Martyr?

YOUR PARTNER DOESN'T take responsibility for their behavior. It doesn't matter what it was or how involved they were in the situation. They will blame someone else for the whole situation. They won't take responsibility for their work, anything that happens in your relationship, or relationships with other people. For example, you walk into your home after work and notice the light won't turn on. As you look around, you realize the power is out. You call your partner and tell ask, "Did you use the money I gave you last week to pay the electric bill? The power is out." Your partner states, "That's not my fault. I spend money on what I want. If you want electricity, you pay the electric bill." You remind them that the money you gave them was specifically for the electric bill and you don't have enough money to cover the bill for another week. They continue to blame you by saying, "It's not my fault you don't make enough money."

YES or NO

3. *Does Your Partner Guilt You?*

TO GET WHAT THEY WANT, your partner will make you feel guilty. They might do this to get money out of you, so you buy something they want or don't leave the relationship. For instance, you are in an argument with your partner and you say, "I just want to feel like you care about my day. I need someone who cares about me as much as I do about them. If your behavior doesn't change, I'm going to leave." In response, they reply, "You can't leave me. I don't know how I would live without you. I am trying to show you how much I love you, but sometimes I don't feel you love me." Statements like this make people feel guilty because they feel ashamed for their behavior. Shame brings feelings of guilt.

YES or NO

4. *Does Your Partner Use Ultimatums?*

ULTIMATUMS ARE USED when your partner wants you to do something. It is a form of manipulation that will focus on your emotions in order to get the job done. For instance, if your partner wants you to stay home with them instead of going out with your friends. You are excited to hang out with your friend because it's been a few months. Plus, you have been planning this get together for weeks. Your friend is only in town for a few more days, and you aren't sure you will be able to see each other otherwise. As you are explaining this to your partner, they tell you, "I've had a bad day and really need you. If you leave, don't bother coming back because you've just proven to me that you don't care. I need someone who cares for me."

YES or NO

5. Does Your Partner Use Your Caring Nature Against You?

ENERGY VAMPIRES WILL spend all the time they can with you because they constantly need to drain you of your energy. When you become emotionally exhausted, it is hard to take the time to focus on treating other people with compassion because you become easily irritated. You won't realize they are draining you dry, but you might start thinking, "If I didn't have to do this all the time for them, I wouldn't feel so tired." There are dozens of ways they will drain you of your compassion. For example, they will stay close to you when you are out with others to take as much energy from you as possible. They will also ask you to do certain things for them because they know you feel bad when you tell them "no."

Yes or NO

6. Does Your Partner Make You Feel Drained?

WHILE YOU MIGHT NOT realize this at first, you might start to notice that you feel better when you are not around your partner. At first, this might make you feel bad. But, once you start to think about it, you realize you have more energy. You aren't as tired and you are more compassionate toward other people–in a way, it is like you are a bit of your old self again.

Energy vampires take as much out of you as they can. They specifically focus on your positive emotions because this is what they need for themselves. One of the main ways they do this is through manipulation and talking at you instead of with you. It's natural for people to feel more emotionally drained when they are being directed to do something or act a certain way. It takes more of our energy to focus. We also feel more stressed because we want to make sure we help them. When people talk with you, you are feeding off each other's energy, which creates more of an internal balance.

YES or NO

7. Do They Constantly Complain About Their Problems?

ENERGY VAMPIRES AREN'T positive people. They will feed off your positivity, but this doesn't mean they will start to become positive. Take a moment to think about when you start talking to a friend or your partner. Do you share positive situations over negative? Usually, people want to open up about the good situations in their life. Energy vampires won't do this. It seems like they are always complaining and don't feel that anything good is happening in their life. If you find yourself agreeing with your partner while they are ranting and complaining on a daily basis, your partner is more than likely an energy vampire.

YES or NO

8. Does Your Partner Put Fear into You?

ENERGY VAMPIRES WILL often put the fear into people. In fact, one way they are able to control their partner well is because they make them fear what will happen if they don't listen. This doesn't mean that all energy vampires are violent. Fear can come in the form of violence, threats, glares, and bullying. For example, you will only order anything from Amazon during certain days and times because you need to make sure when the package arrives, your partner isn't home. Every time they see you ordered something from Amazon, they start yelling. They tell you that you don't know how to handle money and are going to cause money problems. Even when you try to tell them that the item was only a few dollars, they don't want to hear it.

YES or NO

9. Is Your Partner Codependent?

CODEPENDENCY IS A RELATIONSHIP where you act a certain way in order to get a certain behavior from the other person. People who are codependent will often use manipulation and emotions to elicit the responses. For example, your partner might bring you flowers when they want something from you. They might also ignore you if you did something they don't like. For instance, if you decided to go out with your friends instead of staying home and watching a movie with your partner, they ignore you until you apologize and say you won't do something like that again.

YES or NO

10. Do You Feel Like Your Own Worst Enemy?

DO YOU FEEL LIKE YOU can't do anything right? Does your partner usually tell you what you are doing wrong and how you should change your behavior to make them happier? Energy vampires criticize, bully, and tear down their partner's self-esteem to gain control over them. This will lead to self-criticizing and anxiety. You will start to worry that you aren't doing something right. Many people start thinking to themselves, "If I do this, what will my partner think?" When you make a mistake, it is the worst thing in the world because you have made your partner unhappy.

YES or NO

11. Do You Feel Confused by Your Partner's Actions?

ENERGY VAMPIRES CAN make an empath feel very confused. If you feel this way after spending time with your significant other, they might be an energy vampire. This happens because they have taken so many of your emotions that you are left feeling unbalanced. This also happens because their actions don't always make sense. For example, they will bully you and then bring you flowers on the same night.

YES or NO

12. Does Your Partner Have a Lot of Drama?

DRAMA TENDS TO FOLLOW energy vampires. It doesn't matter who they are with or what happens, there is always some sort of drama. Energy vampires tend to start their own drama and then try to find someone to fix what they started. Once you came into the picture, you became this person. They would come to you and ask you to come up with a solution to their problem in their own way. Because energy vampires rarely ask people to help them directly, they will usually say something like, "I don't deserve what is happening to me."

As an empath, your heart begins to break as you want to help them. Therefore, you decide to do whatever you can to help them through their situation. At first, you do this without thinking too much about it. But once your partner starts sucking your energy, you begin to feel frustrated and tired of fixing their problems all the time. However, you find yourself doing what you can to help them until you leave take a stand or leave the relationship.

YES or NO

Your Results

EACH OF THE TWELVE questions focuses on a trait of an energy vampire or how it can affect you. While you might not have circled "yes" to each question, your partner could still be an energy vampire. You might not notice some of the characteristics discussed in this quiz. You might be blind to some of the situations you face on a daily basis.

If you have taken this quiz and are coming to the conclusion that you are in a toxic relationship, the best step you can take right now is to take time for yourself. Coming to terms with the fact that your partner is narcissistic is difficult to process. You will need time. You will also continuously wonder if you are correct in your thinking. Unfortunately, you are, especially if your instincts agree with your thinking.

If you are wondering what to do next, this is completely up to you. You might evaluate your relationship and wonder if it is time to leave. You might think of ways to talk to your partner about your results. While it is difficult, there are some narcissists who want to establish a healthier inner balance and peace of mind. Whatever you do, you need to make sure you are safe and ready for your next step.

Chapter 7: What Is Codependency?

ONE OF THE BEST WAYS to think about codependency is to think of two people within a relationship who need each other in order to function. This can happen in any type of relationship, at least for a period of time. In a healthy relationship, people depend on each other to help the relationship work. In a toxic relationship, people depend on each other in order to help themselves. This is especially true for a narcissistic, as they will only be in a relationship for their benefit.

It is also worth mentioning that your toxic relationship doesn't need to be codependent. You also need to be aware that empathy and codependency are not the same. As an empath, you don't need someone else to function. You become friends and get to know people to help them heal from a traumatic experience. Empathy is a gift. Codependency happens when two people start to lose a bit of their independence–however, you can always gain it back.

If you suspect that codependency is a part of your life that you are coping with and would like to learn more, please refer to my companion book on the subject titled, "Am I Codependent?," by myself, Kara Lawrence. This chapter will cover codependency briefly to give you a rundown, and more information is available if you need it.

Signs of a Codependent Relationship

ONE OF THE BEST WAYS to understand codependency is to know its signs. Because every relationship is different, there are dozens of signs. For the purpose of this book, I am discussing some of the most common signs found in a codependent relationship.

You Have Low Self-Esteem

GOING INTO THE RELATIONSHIP, you knew your self-worth. You were confident, and you believed you could accomplish anything you set your mind to. Now, you are in the middle of a relationship, and you are struggling to believe in yourself. Your work performance is suffering, and you don't take care of yourself like you used to. You find yourself sleeping more as you become frustrated with your state of mind. Sometimes, you feel you are depressed because you don't believe you have become this person. You don't know how you became this person. You know this isn't you, but you can't seem to find the person you once were.

You find yourself depending on your partner to help increase your self-esteem. While this might not happen, you look for any sign that they care about you and support you in order to focus on. Unfortunately, in a toxic relationship, you won't be able to build your self-esteem until you find the courage to leave. Your self-esteem will continue to weaken as you continue to try to find a way to piece your self-worth back together.

You Strive for Control

IN A NARCISSISTIC RELATIONSHIP, you unknowingly give up a lot of control to the narcissist. This will create a need to find more control because people need to feel in control of their lives. When they feel control, they feel secure. Security is a basic human need that makes us feel better. With the loss of security, we start to feel negatively about ourselves and can suffer from anxiety and depression.

You will look toward various avenues in life to find control. For example, you might find yourself controlling what you eat. You might only eat vegetables and fruits as you are trying to lose weight, or you might binge eat.

Your Relationship Lack Communication

WHEN IT COMES TO THIS sign, it is important to realize that nearly every relationship lacks communication at one time or another. This might be because someone forgot to explain something, or it might be because someone is afraid to explain a situation. When you are in a toxic relationship, you might realize that you never had strong communication with your partner. This is because narcissists are exceptional at putting on a mask in order to hide how they really act and what their true intentions are, at least at first. Once they become comfortable, they will start to take off their mask– if only for a brief moment. But, in that moment, you will be able to see their true self. This is usually when an empath starts to realize what type of relationship they are a part of.

Lack of communication happens when people struggle to talk and come to agreements. For an empath, this happens when they become uncomfortable in the relationship or afraid. A narcissist never really learns to communicate well because they are too focused on themselves.

There Is a Need for Approval

YOU WILL LOOK FOR YOUR partner as you need to feel they approve of you. You might ask them certain questions, such as "What do you think of this?" or "Do you like this?" to see their reaction. If they don't approve, you will move on to find something they will approve of.

Turning to your partner to approve is a slippery slope because you are devaluing yourself. You are focused more on making sure your partner is happy with what you are doing than yourself. You will also have a need for approval as it will help ease your fears of abandonment. You feel if your partner approves of your behavior and what you are doing, they won't leave you.

Painful Emotions and Dark Thoughts

PEOPLE IN CODEPENDENT relationships are not as happy as they think they are. In fact, they might not be happy at all. In a toxic relationship, you will struggle with painful emotions that can lead to dark thoughts. These thoughts aren't always about harming yourself. They can also focus on your low self-esteem as you continue to put yourself down. You will tell yourself that you won't amount to anything or you will never be able to make your partner happy.

I want to take this time to give you a very important message: if you are suffering from dark thoughts that include harming yourself or someone else, please reach out for help. If you aren't comfortable going to someone you know, there are a variety of online websites and support groups that will allow you to reach out for help. You have a lot of value and people who love you. Your health and life matters. Do what you need to do to take care of yourself, so you can find your happy and healthy place within this world again.

You Struggle with Boundaries

DEPENDING ON SOMEONE else means you aren't going to understand where your boundary line is unless they help you with it. You won't trust yourself enough to ensure that you are following your boundaries or that the boundaries are best for the relationship. Furthermore, depending on your state of mind, you might struggle to even care that you are enforcing your boundaries. You might ask yourself, "Am I sure I am setting up the best boundaries?" or "How can I successfully enforce my boundaries?"

You Are In a Codependent Relationship, Now What?

IT'S IMPORTANT TO EVALUATE your relationship before you think about what steps come after realizing you are in a codependent relationship. For example, if you also realize your partner is narcissistic, it will probably be best to think about leaving your relationship than trying to fix the codependency. A narcissist is not going to try to work on fixing their relationship because they don't think anything is wrong with them–it's all you. However, if you want to try to work on becoming more independent yourself as you feel it will give you the courage to walk out of your relationship, here are some steps to consider.

You Won't Always Be Codependent

ONCE YOU REALIZE THAT you are codependent, you can change your behavior. You won't always be codependent. It won't be easy and you will need to have patience. However, with dedication, believing in yourself, and working hard, you will be able to reach your ideal state of independence within your relationship. Of course, you can also work on gaining back your independence once you leave your relationship. You don't have to be in a relationship to heal your codependency.

Always Look at Therapy

WHETHER IT IS INDIVIDUAL or couples counseling, you always want to consider talking to a therapist. They can help you understand why you become dependent on your relationship. They can also help you find strategies to reclaim the independence you once had. They can help you strengthen your emotions and help you heal as well.

There can be a lot of social stigma when it comes to counseling. When you are struggling with a negative mindset, this can make you feel uneasy about going or ashamed to seek help. Always remember, it takes courage to admit that you need help and reach out for help. You should never be ashamed to seek help to get your positive mindset back on track. Be proud of the steps you are taking to make sure you are mentally, emotionally, and physically happy, healthy, well-balanced, and at peace.

Make Sure You Have Time Alone

DO WHAT YOU NEED TO take the time to be alone. This might mean you schedule it during your day. It might also mean that you talk to your therapist about how to focus on yourself. Some empaths can struggle when it comes to taking time alone because they feel guilty. You might need to give yourself permission to take alone time. You can do this by telling yourself or writing, "It is okay to take some time for myself. It is healthy and will help me focus on a positive state of mind. I will reach a feeling of internal peace and be able to help people as I am recharged and balanced."

Reconnect to Your Family and Friends

THERE ARE MANY REASONS you mind find yourself losing connection with your family and friends in a toxic relationship. This might be because when you become codependent, you isolate yourself from other people. You might also lose connection because your partner controlled who you talked to and who you didn't. Whatever the reason for losing touch with your support system is, you need to make sure you reconnect with them. They will be able to help you through this difficult time. They will also try to understand as you as they want to do what they can to help you find a mentally stable and happy place again.

It doesn't matter how you connect with them. If you aren't comfortable calling them at first, then send them a text or email. It might take time to start reconnecting with some people. The key is to try and see how everything unfolds. The people in your life who truly love and care for you will always find the time to reconnect and help you in tough situations.

Chapter 8: Setting Boundaries and Enforcing Them

"CREATE BOUNDARIES. Honor your limits. Say no. Take a break. Let go. Stay grounded. Nurture your body. Love your vulnerability. And if all else fails, breathe deeply." — Aletheia Luna (Walter, 2019).

Boundaries are not always easy to set, and they can be even harder to enforce. Part of this reason is that boundaries are invisible. This makes it easier for people to bend their boundaries when it comes to certain people or situations. Unfortunately, this can also lead people down a difficult path. The good news is, you are always able to learn how to set and enforce boundaries.

Setting Boundaries

IT WILL BE UP TO YOU to set any boundaries between you and a narcissist. This is because narcissists are not capable of setting boundaries due to their high opinion of themselves. They don't believe that anyone would want to set boundaries with them. A narcissist feels you should always want to be around them and allow them to do what they want. Furthermore, don't like it when someone gives them limits because this is a form of control. You aren't supposed to control the narcissist; they are supposed to control you.

One of the most important steps you can take as you start to set boundaries is to take it one step at a time. You are going to struggle with the narcissist, especially at first. They are going to try to use several strategies to break the boundaries. To keep your mind at peace, you should work on one or two boundaries at the time. You can find out which boundaries are the best to start by creating a list. Write down what you need to maintain a healthy mindset. If you are still in a relationship with a narcissist, you will need to communicate everything with them. Unfortunately, this might not go well, which can cause more problems in your relationship.

It's important to realize that you don't just want to set boundaries if you are involved in a toxic relationship. You also want to set boundaries as they will help you stay out of another toxic relationship.

There are a variety of tips for setting boundaries. I am going to focus on some of the most well-known tips that work for narcissists and will help you stay out of a toxic relationship.

This Is Not a One Time Situation

ONE OF THE FIRST STEPS you need to follow when setting boundaries is that you will be doing it constantly with a narcissist. You won't be able to sit down with them, explain the boundaries, and expect them to follow each boundary. Narcissists aren't going to be able to comprehend boundaries and how you are enforcing them.

This can make establishing boundaries a little more difficult because of your highly sensitive nature. For example, the narcissist is going to make you feel guilty. They know what buttons they need to push to get what they want, and they will do as much pushing as they want. This can cause you to fall back into a vicious cycle with the narcissist if you aren't careful. You need to do your best to remember that your mental health is important, and the strategies they are using to try to get their way is part of their personality disorder. Do you best to stay calm, take time to maintain a peaceful mind, and have a strong support group that can help you during the tough times.

Know Where the Lines Are Drawn

BOUNDARIES ESTABLISH invisible lines that are hard for both parties to see and understand. As you become calmer and feel more at peace, you can find yourself starting to slack on the boundaries. You might catch yourself thinking, "It's okay if they do this, it's not going to hurt me anymore. I feel better." The reality is, once you allow the narcissist to cross the line, they are going to continue to push, and you will soon find yourself in the same situation.

Before you put the boundary into motion, know what you want and what you don't want. Write all this information down if it will help you keep your mind on the drawn line. For example, you are thinking of the behaviors you put up with from your partner. You decide what behaviors you will tolerate and what behaviors you will not. You decide that you will no longer put up with their bullying behavior, so you tell your partner, "I will not put up with your name-calling, bullying, or putting me down in any way. You need to respect me as your partner. If you don't follow this, I will end the conversation, leave the area, and come back when I feel we can discuss the situation civilly."

You Don't Need to Share Everything

NARCISSISTS ARE GOOD at interrogating people. They want to know everything about you and the situation as this helps them maintain their control. No matter what tactic they try on you, the best advice to remember in this situation is that you don't have to share anything you don't want to. If you feel the information they are asking for is going to give them ammunition to hold against you, don't share it. Don't answer their questions or try to shift the conversation onto something else.

Don't Continue If You Are Not Comfortable

THERE ARE A LOT OF behaviors that will make you uncomfortable when you are with a narcissist. For example, they might belittle you or embarrass you in front of other people. If you find yourself in an uncomfortable situation, don't continue the conversation. In fact, some people say you shouldn't even respond. A narcissist tends to continue behaviors when they are given a reaction. Therefore, if you don't react, they will eventually stop with that behavior.

This can be hard for an empath because of the mix of emotions you will hold within you. You will start to feel overwhelmed, which can create more struggles. At the same time, if you are in a public setting, you will try to hold everything in. Of course, this can only make the situation worse because you will continue to absorb energy. As an empath, you always need to do what you can to help control your emotions, no matter what environment you are in. If you find yourself in this situation, take a moment to step outside or in a different room where you can be alone for a few minutes. Try to sort through your emotions, use meditation, or breathing exercises to help get rid of some negative emotions.

Another technique to use in an uncomfortable situation is to talk about something the narcissist cares about. This will get the narcissist on a different topic and can give you a break from the uncomfortable situation.

State What They Are Doing In a Matter of Fact Way

CALLING THE NARCISSIST out on their behavior is helpful when it comes to setting and maintaining boundaries, but there are empaths that will struggle with this step. It's okay if you are uncomfortable telling the narcissist, "You are bullying me" or "You are putting me down, and that isn't right." You might worry about this step because of their response. The key factor to remember is their response doesn't matter. You don't have to say anything else after you have called them out on their behavior. All you need to do is stand up for yourself and not allow yourself to bend if they try anything.

Have an Escape Plan

NARCISSISTS WILL TRY multiple strategies to get what they want. If they notice that their usual routine isn't working, they will try to find something that will. For example, if you used to bend to their needs out of guilt, but this no longer works, they might try bullying you. They might feel that a more aggressive approach will get you to do what they want. It's important to make sure that you don't bend your boundaries, no matter what strategy they try to use. One way to help you follow your boundaries is to develop an escape plan. This might be you leave the room if they don't stop belittling you after you ask them to.

There are many ways you can leave a conversation when you are not comfortable. For instance, you can be direct or make up an excuse, such as you need to be somewhere, or you need to call someone. One of the most important factors to remember is that you never need anyone's permission to leave an uncomfortable situation. You need to worry about your mental health, so get up and go if you don't like the conversation or how your partner is acting.

Enforcing Boundaries

SOME OF THE TECHNIQUES we discussed previously are always ways that will help you enforce your boundaries. For instance, walking out of the room when your partner is making you uncomfortable or doesn't follow the boundaries will enforce them. Of course, there are many other techniques available to help you keep your boundaries exactly where they should be.

Consistency

IT'S ALWAYS IMPORTANT to be consistent when you are enforcing boundaries. This will not only help you, but it will also help the narcissist realize you aren't going to bend for them anymore. This doesn't mean they will give up trying, but it does mean that they are starting to back away. Depending on where you are in your relationship, if you are still in one, it will depend on how you handle the relationship from this moment.

But the best step you can take is continuing to remain consistent with your boundaries.

No Means No

A LOT OF PEOPLE STRUGGLE with the word "no." People struggle to understand the word, and people struggle to say the word. As an empath, you will struggle to say and enforce the word no. In fact, you probably already realize you do this. You say "no" and find yourself feeling guilty because all the person did was ask for a little help. Why couldn't you help them? You start thinking if it really would have been too much of a burden to agree to help them. We don't often think, "I said no because I am emotionally exhausted and need to take care of myself" or "I am allowed to say no when I am not comfortable helping someone."

A narcissist knows that you struggle to enforce the word no. They know that you already feel guilty, so they can easily make you feel even more guilty. They will try anything to get you to change your mind once they hear you say the word no. I understand it's not always easy but saying "no" will also help you feel better. You will start to feel less stressed, you will be able to create a better internal balance, and you will feel better.

You never need to explain why you said no. In fact, think of the word as a full sentence. You don't need to open up and tell anyone your reasoning. You don't even need to think of a reason.

Your Boundaries Are Non-Negotiable

DON'T NEGOTIATE YOUR boundaries with anyone. Once you ask for someone's advice, you are starting to give away your control with your boundaries. Eventually, you will find yourself allowing people to cross the imaginary line, and the cycle will continue. You need to take time to evaluate your emotional and mental health, what problems you are having in your relationship, and what you want out of the relationship. You need to focus on making yourself happy, no one else.

Don't Apologize for Your Boundaries

AS AN EMPATH, YOU APOLOGIZE a lot. I know exactly how this goes as an empath myself. You start to feel bad, or you are so afraid of hurting the other person's feelings that you start your sentences with an apology. You will say, "I'm sorry, but I can't help you right now." Then, you might add another "I'm sorry" because you still feel bad about not being able to help. After all, you are an empath and are supposed to help whenever someone needs it, right? No, you always need to take care of yourself first.

I know this is easier said than done. I remember when I came to this conclusion. I was sitting in my grass with my back against the wall of my home and thinking about how I just texted my friend to tell her I couldn't come over before her son's birthday party to help her decorate. I had my reasons, but at the same time, I knew there was going to be a lot of people, and I just couldn't bring myself to be there an extra two hours.

Looking back, I apologized to her in three different text messages. Each time she would tell me that it was fine not to worry about it, she had enough help. Part of this just made me feel worse because she is such a great friend and I felt like I wasn't. As I sat there with the sun beating down on me, I thought "No, I am not going to allow myself to feel bad. I need to take care of me. There is no reason for me to apologize to anyone for taking care of me." At that moment, I vowed to apologize less and take care of myself more. I am not going to tell you it happened easily. In fact, I still catch myself apologizing for situations I don't need to and neglecting my mindset from time to time. But the point is, I catch myself and I am working on it. I am working on keeping my boundaries and enforcing them. It's possible, and I know you can follow the same path.

Are you enjoying this book? Please consider leaving it a review!

Chapter 9: If I'm an Empath, Why Didn't I Sense a Narcissist?

BY NOW, YOU ARE PROBABLY wondering, "If I can feel someone's emotions and I know things, why didn't I sense a narcissist?"

One of the main factors I have noticed since I started to enforce my boundaries is I have stronger senses. I pay more attention to the red flags, which helped me realize when a narcissist is in my path. I wasn't always able to sense a narcissist right away. As empaths, we need to work on enhancing our senses. This is one of the reasons you might not have sensed a narcissist; your senses are not as strong as they can be. Of course, there are many other reasons, and there is usually a number of reasons why you didn't notice your partner is a narcissist right away.

One of the straight to the point answers is that you were blinded by your emotions and your belief you could help them. You might have been caught up in love or you might have pushed your feelings aside because you saw someone who needed your help. However, the real answer holds several parts and is more complex than this.

How Strong Is Your Connection?

THE FIRST QUESTION you need to think of is how strongly are you connected to your empathic abilities. If you were in the toxic relationship years ago, think back to how strong your gifts were when you first got into the relationship. It's important to know this as it will help you distinguish part of your puzzle. For instance, if you didn't completely understand your empathic abilities or you didn't pay a lot of attention to them, you probably didn't notice the feelings you received from the narcissist.

There is nothing wrong with this. In fact, there is nothing wrong with any reason for not sensing a narcissist or ignoring your emotions. It's all a part of life as an empath. When our connection isn't strong, we need to take time to strengthen our abilities so we come to understand the special gift we've been given.

Your Need to Help Is Powerful

AS A NARCISSIST, YOU have a powerful feeling to help other people. This need can often feel like a craving you can't get rid of. On top of this, the more you help people, the more you realize you want to help more people. If you are not careful, you can become overwhelmed by this need, which can lead you into toxic relationships because you want to help absolutely everyone you can.

The empathic gift is similar to every other gift people have. You need to have boundaries, follow through with these boundaries, and take care of yourself to remain at a healthy level. If you allow yourself, without your knowledge, to become unhealthy, you are going to struggle to find an emotional balance. When this happens, you feel off and you can even feel like you are not contributing to this world. Therefore, you are going to strive to help other people because it makes you feel good. The person you help doesn't matter. Sometimes you will try to help people who don't want your help, which is usually the case when it comes to a narcissist.

This is nothing to be ashamed about. Learning your boundaries is all part of being an empath.

You Weren't Paying Attention to the Signs

MANY PEOPLE REFER TO the signs as the "red flags" of narcissism. I have already talked about these red flags and examples of these flags are throughout the pages of this book. These signs are what makes a narcissist who they are. They are the controlling behavior, manipulative tactics, and the need to talk about themselves.

It's hard to notice something bad about the person you feel is your soulmate, especially in the beginning of the relationship. You feel that you are in a fairy and that dreams do come true. Unfortunately, this is not a Disney movie and your relationship is going to have problems as every relationship does.

Don't talk down to yourself if you realize you didn't notice the signs because you thought you were in love. Instead, use this opportunity to grow as an empath. Look at what boundaries you can establish to protect yourself for the next time a narcissist is in your path. Look at how you can become more mindful of your environment and the people around you, so you are more likely to notice the signs.

You Didn't Understand Narcissism

ANOTHER REASON IS BECAUSE you didn't truly understand narcissism. This is a common reason because there is more to narcissism than someone who talks highly about themselves constantly. In fact, some narcissists don't follow this method as much as others. They would rather hear other people talk highly about them than themselves. Therefore, they will use certain manipulation tactics to get people to start talking. The more you educate yourself about narcissism and the magnetic attraction to empaths have to narcissist, the more you will be able to notice when a narcissist is talking to you.

But the Biggest Reason of Them All: Manipulation

NARCISSISTS ARE PROFESSIONALS when it comes to manipulation. This is when a narcissist gets the empath to change their behavior through certain techniques. For example, making you feel guilty for saying no is a form of manipulation. The narcissist is trying to get you to change your mind and do what they want you to do by making you feel guilty. There are dozens of manipulation tactics, but here are some of the most common that you should watch out for.

Shaming

A NARCISSIST WILL MAKE you feel ashamed of your behavior. They might do this in front of other people, including your family and friends, or when you are alone. A narcissist doesn't care how they make you feel. What they care about is that you follow their orders. For instance, you are out with a couple of friends, and you decide to go play pool with your friends. After you get back to your table, your partner looks at you and says, "The next time you go and play pool without me, try not to flaunt anything in front of other guys." You look at your partner as you feel your face become warm. You are embarrassed but also confused because you didn't even talk to anyone else except for your friend. Your partner doesn't care who you talked to or who you didn't. What they care about is that you don't go off and play pool without them.

One of the dangers of shaming is that you don't always realize it is happening. For example, you tell your partner, "I didn't talk to anyone, and I definitely didn't flaunt anything." To get you to change your perspective, they will say, "I was just kidding. Relax." Of course, this can make you feel more embarrassed because now you look like you can't even take a joke–which is their point. They want you to feel this way as it leverages more control over your emotions.

One main reason a narcissist will look to shaming people is because it is a way to make you feel weak. This gives them power over you as you start to question yourself. You start to believe that you were flaunting it in front of other people or that you can't take a joke. They will make you question yourself.

They will Act Like the Victim

YOU PARTNER COMES HOME from work and starts ranting about their boss. They are angry because their boss told them that they are showing poor work performance and are now on work probation. If they don't improve their performance within a few months, they will be let go. They start taking their anger out on you as they say, "If you would do more around here, I wouldn't be so stressed at work. Why are you so lazy?" You tell your partner that you work just to come home to cook and clean. You then remind them that they don't pick up after themselves, which leaves you to do it. In response, your partner says, "You just don't understand me. Why can't you just be on my side and support me?"

You will have many conversations and arguments that end up with your partner acting like the victim. Even if you are trying to tell them how you feel, they will turn it toward them. You will become confused because their victimization won't make sense to you, but it doesn't have to. It is a manipulation tactic to try to get you to give them sympathy.

They will Act Like a Savior

"THESE PICTURE FRAMES in the living room are crooked. I told you to check when you clean the house. Come on! Don't be stupid!!" —A narcissistic husband to his wife (Ni, 2019).

You might have heard something similar to the above quote. This is because it follows a common manipulation tactic that makes them seem like you need them. You won't be able to clean the house correctly if you didn't have them telling you how to clean the house. While you will see them as controlling and disrespectful, they will see themselves as your savior. They will also start to make you believe this is true. The more a narcissist tells you comments like the one above, the more they will lower your self-esteem. If this happens too much, you will start to believe that they are right, you do need them in order to do simple tasks.

Chapter 10: Escaping the Toxic Relationship and Recovering

THIS CHAPTER WILL COVER your escape from a toxic relationship, potentially an abusive one. If you feel you would like to hear more information about narcissistic abuse, I have written an entire book on the subject that you are welcome to refer to titled, "Invisible Abuse," It covers in depth the covert manipulation and abuse tactics of Narcissists and how to defend against them.

There are many reasons you chose to read this book. You might have placed this book in your cart because you wanted to understand the connection between narcissists and empaths. You might have clicked on this book because you want to heal from your toxic past by understanding the connection better. You also might be here because you are still in a toxic relationship and not sure how to get out. Whatever the reason is, this chapter is here to help you whether you need to escape and heal or just heal.

To those of who you still need to escape, I want you to know that I understand what you are going through. I understand the fear, worry, and how much courage you need to build before you are able to make the leap. This is a difficult time in your life, but I know you have the strength to leave your toxic environment. I know that you can overcome this challenge, heal, and become a better person because of it. No matter where you are emotionally and mentally sitting at this moment, you have the power and you are special.

To those of you who have left but are still healing, I understand you as well. I am proud of you for taking the step and know how hard it is to heal. You are an amazing person who is full of courage, and you will continue to overcome this difficult time in your life. I know that you still have a lot of questions and just because you are no longer in the relationship doesn't mean you aren't suffering. Never forget the strength you hold. You have already taken a huge step to change your life. Continue to walk down your path with your head held high.

Ending a Toxic Relationship

ENDING A RELATIONSHIP is not an easy step. However, it can become even worse when you are in a toxic relationship. There are other factors that often contribute to the need to leave. For instance, you could be in a mentally, physically, or emotionally abusive relationship.

When you are trying to leave your toxic relationship with a narcissist, there are going to be certain factors you include into leaving the relationship. For instance, for your safety you might need to leave when they are not present. While you never want to leave a relationship without informing your significant other, this might not be possible in the relationship you are in. On the flip side, you might try to end the relationship, but find that your partner is in denial. They don't believe that you will take the step to leave them. Remember, a narcissist thinks they are the most important person in the world–why would you leave them?

No matter what you story is, here are some steps to take when escaping from a toxic relationship.

Get Out of the Denial Phase

IT DOESN'T MATTER IF you are the one trying to leave or not, there is still a denial phase and you need to get over this phase to end your relationship. You're going to find yourself in denial for many reasons. One of the reasons for this is because people have the belief that if you leave someone you loved, you never truly loved them. This can make people feel like they were fooled or that love doesn't exist. However, this is also a myth. You can leave someone that you loved. The fact is, you love yourself more. This isn't saying that you are a narcissist yourself. It is saying that you value your self-care. You can love someone and still refuse to live the way they want you to live or allow them to treat you poorly. Another reason is because it's hard to let go. We don't want to believe that this is really the end. The fact is, if you feel this way, you do love them, but you are not willing to put up with factors of the relationship.

As you step off the boat of denial, it's going to be emotionally painful and draining. This is a phase that no one likes to go through but is part of the process. It's also one of the first steps of healing. You are coming to terms with everything. At this point, you are going to ask yourself dozens of questions, such as, "Does my significant other drain me?" "Do I feel loved?" "Do I truly love them?" "Are they able to change?" "Is our relationship give and take or am I just giving?" The questions you answer are going to be general and also focus directly on your relationship. Take time to think about the questions you have. You might find it helpful to write them down and add your answers and emotions to them. You need to reflect in order to separate your emotions and start healing.

Know What the Perks Are

THIS MIGHT SOUND LIKE a step backward, but it is going to be helpful in your process. First, you always want to do your best to remain positive, no matter what is going on. This is going to be harder under some circumstances, but it will help you heal through depression, sadness, or any type of emotion.

No matter what relationship you are in, there were good times. Think of those times. Think of what your significant other does for you. A narcissist will not do much for you, but there are a couple of situations they might help you with. For example, they may have helped you learn that you need to take care of yourself. A narcissist can often help people find a balance between taking care of other people and themselves. However, they usually don't realize they are doing it. You will sometimes learn this balance a bit more naturally as you start to release the negativity, they bring you or see the healthy ways they take care of themselves.

You can figure this out by asking yourself a series of questions, just like you did in the last step. For example, does your significant other make you feel attractive? Do you enjoy watching movies together? Don't be ashamed or afraid to think of the perks. They exist, otherwise you wouldn't have stayed in the relationship.

Write Down Your Emotions

NOT ONLY DO YOU WANT to pay attention to your emotions, but it will be helpful to write them down. First, this is always something to do when you are struggling to understand your emotions or trying to separate your emotions from other people's emotions. While you can always take the time to write about your emotions as they are happening, do it as soon as you can. You can always use a notepad or other downloadable app on your phone that will allow you to type them out. You can also write everything out in an email to yourself or set up a Google Docs account. This will allow you to use your phone to write and retrieve it on your computer. Of course, there is always paper and pen.

Another reason you should start writing down your emotions is because it can help you heal. One of the greatest benefits about writing is it helps you heal emotionally and mentally. Along with writing down your emotions, you can take time to write about your day. Reflect on your relationship if you are having trouble leaving and try to find out why. What is keeping you tied to your significant other, even though they hurt you so much? Sometimes we can find it hard to start writing, especially about something that is affecting us so much. However, once you start writing the first few words, you will have trouble putting your pen, phone, or laptop down.

Fill in Your Void

LEAVING A RELATIONSHIP is going to create a hole in your heart and life. It is going to take a while to fill this void, which is why one of the best steps you can take is starting before you exit your relationship. First, this is going to help you find the courage to leave. You will start to depend on yourself to fill in any voids you have in your life instead of looking for other people to do it for you.

To do this, make a list of 5, 10, 15, or 20 self-care ideas, hobbies, or anything you can do that might help fill the void.

You don't want to make yourself so busy that you are ignoring your emotions. You simply want to help yourself become whole again while maintaining a mindful attitude.

An example list might look like this:

1. Take time to write for a half hour every day.
2. Meditate for 10 minutes every morning.
3. When needed, do a little retail therapy with a friend.
4. Go out for coffee with friends.
5. Learn how to make my own jewelry.
6. Cuddle up with my pets and be grateful for my time with them.
7. Listen to songs that speak to me and allow my tears to flow.
8. Join a gym and take time to exercise three to four times a week.
9. Get out in nature, such as go for a walk on a country road or a hike.
10. Go to the lakes and allow the sound and warmth of the sun to heal my soul.

Hang Out with Positive Friends and Family

YOU HAVE PROBABLY HEARD the phrase that you start to act like the people you hang out with. While you always maintain your individuality, there is a lot of truth to this statement. If you hang out with people who are negative, you are going to be more negative. On the flip side, if you hang out with people who are positive, then you will become more positive. The foundation of this step is to surround yourself with people who will bring positivity to your life, especially when you are struggling with a negative situation.

Notice your friends and family that bring you the most happiness and support. Think of the once who are able to find the positives in every negative situation. In fact, you probably already have several people that come to your mind. Then again, you might only have a few. Let's face it, as empaths we are typically introverted and would rather have a few close friends than several. The point is–take in some of their positivity.

Write Yourself Little Notes

ONE OF THE BEST WAYS we maintain positivity is by reading something that is positive. It doesn't matter if it is from ourselves or someone else. Buy a bunch of sticky notes and write yourself little notes that you will post around your home, car, office, or anywhere you will be at daily. I understand you will want to be a little more discreet if you are living with your significant other and still trying to leave them. We all have places our significant other doesn't go or look at often. You might also feel the best is to have these little notes in a Word document on your laptop, Google Docs, or on your phone. You need to do what's best and safest for you.

The notes can say anything positive you want them to. You can write "You are amazing!" "You got this!" "You are intelligent" "Be proud of yourself" "You are loved." Write whatever you need to write to get into a more positive mindset. The more positive your mindset is, the easier it will be to maintain the courage to leave and heal.

Have a Safe Place to Go

THIS ISN'T THE MOST positive part of the escaping process, but it is necessary. Narcissists can become abusive in many ways. It is important that you know where you are going to go when you leave and that you will be safe. If you know this can become a dangerous situation, get as many people involved to help you as you can. You don't always need to involve the police, but if you are truly concerned for your safety, it would be a good idea. Don't forget to check out any shelters at the same time. There are a lot of nonprofit organizations that will have resources to help you through this difficult time. They will be able to give you a sense of support and help you heal. It's not easy to focus on ourselves as empaths, but it is necessary. In fact, this becomes more important when times are tough.

Allow Yourself to Heal and Rest

YOU NEED TO MAKE SURE you take time for yourself after leaving a toxic relationship. You need to allow yourself time to recharge and find your balance. This is going to take longer than a normal recharge or balance because you have dealt with a toxic relationship for so long.

While you will be able to find your balance within a few weeks to a couple of months, you will still need to heal. Unfortunately, healing from a toxic relationship can take years. Some people never truly get over it. The key is to take your time. You need to acknowledge your emotions to start the healing process. You also need to do whatever you need to do in order to start healing, such as writing or going to therapy.

Finding the Courage to Leave

THE MAIN STEP IS TO find the courage to leave. Finding enough courage will depend on several factors, such as how long you have been in the relationship. If you are married and have been a part of the relationship for years or decades, it might take time to build up enough courage for you to leave. On the other hand, you might be so fed up with the relationship and your partner that you leave without giving it a second thought.

There are many places you can look for courage. One of the biggest sources of courage will come from your support group. Even if you haven't talked to your parents, siblings, cousins, and friends, they will still want to help you leave a toxic relationship. Through their support, you will feel like you can accomplish this step.

Finding the courage to leave is also going to come from deep within you. You will need to focus on the positive aspects of your life and what you want to accomplish. You can also think of how you want to reach your best self, but your partner will not help you achieve this goal. You will want to focus on building your self-esteem and telling yourself that you are intelligent, compassionate, caring, loving, and have an amazing talent. Tell yourself that you have a great gift as an empath and you will be able to accomplish more than you ever thought possible once you find the courage to leave. There are a variety of ways to find courage. You need to focus on how you can build the courage inside of you. Even if you don't feel that you still have the fire inside of you, it is still there.

Steps to Healing

SOME OF THE WAYS YOU use to help you leave a toxic relationship are some of the same strategies you can use to help yourself heal. For example, you can continue to write in your journal about your healing process. You will also want to continue on filling your void. One of the biggest ways to heal is to focus on getting your life back on track. This is something that can make you feel overwhelmed. For example, you might ask yourself, "How do I start?" or "How can I do this?"

First, you need to do what you can to take it as easy as possible. I know this is easier said than done, but the stress you feel from leaving your relationship and trying to get your life back on track is going to take a toll on your emotions.

Step One: Understand the Stages of Recovery

WHILE RECOVERING FROM a toxic relationship can be different for everyone, there are generally three main states that you will go through as you heal.

Stage One: The "Victim"

During this stage, you might be in denial about your relationship. You will feel rejected, ashamed, hurt, confused, afraid, and abandoned. When it comes to anger, you will be angry at your ex-partner and angry at yourself. You might also be angry at the person who set you two up and supported your relationship. It's important to understand that feeling angry at everyone is a typical part of this stage. Like your other emotions, you need to acknowledge the emotion in order to heal. If you try to push anger or any other emotion to the side, you are going to get stuck in the stage. You will always feel like a victim. You need to work toward feeling like a survivor.

During this stage, you will learn about narcissism and how your relationship came to be. You should also learn that you are not alone. There are millions of people who are survivors and still trying to escape a toxic relationship. If you are in need of support, there are dozens of online communities you can look into. Of course, you might also find local groups that will offer you support as well.

Stage Two: Survivor

When you are in the survivor stage, your emotions and thoughts will start to become more positive. You will be feeling hopeful, less angry, learning how to self-soothe, and learning self-care techniques. At the same time, you will be struggling to rebuild your life. You won't be ready to forgive your ex or yourself yet, and you will find yourself reevaluating other friendships in your life. You will hopefully be getting counseling and working toward regaining trust for other people in your life. It's hard to trust anyone after a toxic relationship.

During this age, you will work on setting boundaries for yourself. You will also need to focus on how you will stick to your boundaries. You also want to work on healing your inner child. For example, you might feel that your parents never allowed you to acknowledge and talk about your emotions. Therefore, you find yourself struggling to do so now. This would be one of your vulnerabilities, which can lead you to another toxic relationship. Take time to heal your inner child. You can do this by visualizing yourself as a child and having a conversation with them. For instance, imagine yourself sitting next to you. You might start to visualize playing with their hair as you tell them what you needed to hear as a child.

You also need to take your life back. Through healing, you will start to focus on your life and goals. You will focus on maintaining financial freedom and focus on creating a healthy social life. When you are in a toxic relationship, you can find yourself becoming distant with friends and family. Once you are free from the relationship, you need to start reconnecting with everyone.

Stage Three: Surthriver

At this stage, you need to focus on how you are still feeling and work toward healing those emotions. It doesn't matter how you are still feeling. You could be feeling angry, embarrassed, like you are being judged by other people, and burdened with thoughts about your relationship. Reevaluate your emotions, so you can focus on the areas that you need to.

During this stage, you should gain increase your self-confidence and self-worth. These are two important factors in our lives that we often struggle with, especially after an unhealthy relationship. Take time to practice self-love and notice your milestones. This is one reason it is great to start a journal. You will be able to look back at how you are progressing over time, which can make you feel like you are truly starting to heal.

You should also work on mindfulness, which is remaining in the moment. The more mindful we are about our environment and the people we talk to, the more we can protect ourselves from another toxic relationship. With mindfulness, your anxiety will start to disappear, you will understand your emotions better, and you will establish a sense of peace in your mind.

Step Two: Get the Toxicity Out of Your System

I DON'T HAVE TO TELL you how toxic your relationship was because you are the one who knows that the best. By now, you also know how dangerous this toxicity is to your psychological, emotional, and physical health. While you won't be able to cleanse your soul in one day, you will be able to see a change within yourself from the first time you focus on cleansing. This can be through journaling, meditation, or taking some time for yourself. You might even look into essential oils and crystals, as there are a lot of ways you can use to help yourself heal.

Step Three: Set Boundaries and Stick to Them

I HAVE ALREADY DISCUSSED this, so I won't go into too much detail about it now. The key is to ensure that whatever boundaries you set, you follow through with them. This isn't going to be easy at first, and you will find yourself struggling. You will start to feel bad when you can't help someone because it crosses your boundaries.

Once you are on the mend, you will start to think, "I can bend it a little, just this once, in order to help someone." This thought will only lead you to fall back into a toxic relationship. You need to remember your boundaries are put in place so you can take care of yourself. Think of them as a protective shield. We all need to protect ourselves as it is part of the self-care plan. There is nothing wrong with sticking to your boundaries, and you should never feel guilty for taking care of yourself.

Step Four: Reflect, Acknowledge, and Forgive

AS YOU REFLECT ON YOUR relationship, ask yourself how it all came to be, acknowledge what happened, and accept your emotions, you also need to forgive yourself. It can be hard for an empath to understand why they let themselves get caught up in a relationship.

When you continue to focus on the "why" and "how," you start to lose focus on healing. One of the main points of healing is you are moving forward and not looking backward. The more you ask yourself, "How could I let this happen?" the more you are looking backward. Instead, you need to reflect, acknowledge, and forgive.

When you are starting to forgive, you need to focus on yourself and your ex-partner. Like healing, forgiveness will take time. Don't try to rush it as you will only become frustrated. You have to let the forgiveness come naturally. You will be able to do this as you take time to recharge and heal.

Step Five: But Part of Me Knew...

YES, CHANCES ARE PART of you did know that they were narcissistic, and you were getting into a toxic relationship. There is always a part of an empath that knows what is going to happen and where they are heading. Take responsibility for the fact that part of you did know. However, you need to be careful that you don't start to blame yourself. There is a big difference between responsibility and self-blame. It's important you don't get them confused.

As you are taking responsibility, think about a plan you can create for yourself, so you don't fall into another toxic relationship. This plan might include learning as much as you can about narcissists, empaths, and how they relate to each other. It might also include writing down signs that you are heading into a toxic relationship. You will then discuss strategies you can use to help keep you away from that path.

Step Six: What Are Your Vulnerabilities?

ONE OF THE KEY REASONS you stayed in a toxic relationship is because the narcissist gave you something that you need. This could be anything from reminding you of how comforting your mother was to help you feel less lonely. Whatever the factors were, you need to acknowledge them, write them down, and try to find ways to help you strengthen your vulnerabilities. For example, if you were looking for security, such as having someone to come home to, reflect on this. Why can't you make yourself feel secure? How could you make yourself feel more secure?

Step Seven: No Contact

AS LONG AS YOU DON'T have any children, don't keep in contact. In fact, many people who have left a narcissistic relationship will tell you that it is best to place a personal "no contact" order in your boundaries. Don't talk to them, don't let them talk to you, and don't let any mutual friends discuss them in your presence. When we maintain contact, we allow the person to continue to hold a part of us, especially as empaths.

You will struggle to control your emotions when they contact you. You will find yourself struggling to forgive. You might have flashbacks which strengthen your internal pain. You might also find yourself struggling if they try to take you back into their lives. One of the best ways to make sure you don't end up in that toxic relationship again is to follow your no contact boundary. Do you best to tell yourself, "I am not mean or disrespectful to someone I once loved. I am allowing myself to heal. I am taking care of myself. I am protecting myself."

Chapter 11: Taking Preventative Measures

"YOU CAN'T CHANGE SOMEONE Who Doesn't See an Issue in Their Actions." – Unknown (Bryan, 2019).

No matter where you are sitting with a narcissist–whether you are still in the relationship, working on leaving, or working on healing you need to take preventative measures. The only person who can truly protect you is you. While other people, such as family and friends will strive to protect you, an individual always has to learn to protect themselves as well. Protecting yourself is a sure way to know you will be able to see red flags and keep yourself out of a toxic relationship.

Do You Act Like Your Best Self In Their Presence?

"I STARTED TO CHANGE, it was like I wasn't myself anymore. I am not sure when or how it happened, but I did start to notice it after a few months." This is a common phrase when it comes to a toxic relationship. This doesn't mean that you start to become drained right away, though you might feel a difference in your energy level. It means that you take part in aspects of your personality you try to control or stay away from. For example, you might find yourself gossiping with this person. As you do this, you might even think "Wait, this isn't me. Why am I saying such mean things about someone I care about?"

Sometimes you become easily irritable and begin to lose patience. One reason for this is due to your loss of energy.

However, other reasons include absorbing the person's emotions and starting to pick up on their personality characteristics. If you are with the person regularly, you will start to act like them from time to time, especially when you are around them.

When you start to pay more attention to your thoughts and actions, in other words, you become mindful, you will catch yourself acting differently quickly. You will then be able to analyze the situation, people you are with, and why are you starting to fall short of acting like your best self. Once you realize that it is because of the narcissist, you will be able to work on removing yourself from any relationship before you get too deep. This doesn't mean you will have an easier time getting the person to stop contacting you. But it does mean you will be able to save yourself from a lot of emotional pain and suffering.

How Do You Feel When You Are with Them?

TAKE TIME TO THINK about how you really feel when you are with them and once you leave their presence. While this can be a challenge if you are starting to fall in love with the person, you will be able to notice a change in your mood and energy levels early, which can help prevent you from continuing into a toxic relationship.

When you are truly falling in love with someone, they make you feel happy, give you a peace of mind, and you feel they care about you. You feel like you are on cloud nine and nothing is able to take you down. They won't drain you of your energy. Instead, they will give you more energy because you are so happy to be in their presence. They give you something else to look forward to every day. On top of this, you don't become anxious in their presence. You don't wonder what their mood will be and you don't become annoyed by them.

When you aren't truly interested in the person, you will become bored from time to time. This might happen when they start to talk about themselves. If you start to notice they make you feel negatively, it is time to evaluate the relationship. What are they doing to make you feel this way? How do you feel? Do they make you feel guilty or ashamed? Do they talk down to you, which is causing you to question yourself?

One of the first ways to tell if you are in the presence of a healthy or unhealthy person is how they make you feel. If you don't feel healthy, your relationship is going to become toxic.

Do They Open Up Your Creativity?

PEOPLE WHO ARE GOOD for you are going to help you succeed. People who aren't good for you are going to do the direct opposite. Even if you don't see yourself as an artist, writer, or feel very creative, you still have creativity in you. This creativity might show up in your work, when you are cooking, or in another activity. When you are heading into the right relationship, you are going to feel more creative. This is because you will feel happier and, in a sense, more alive. If you are heading into a toxic relationship, you are going to close down some of your walls. You are going to lose interest in activities you used to enjoy. This will cause you to close your creativity rather than open it up wider.

Learn From Your Mistakes

THIS ISN'T ALWAYS EASY. I have made mistakes repeatedly because I didn't learn the first time. It happens to everyone. Learning from your mistakes, especially as an empath, takes a certain mindset because we tend to feel bad about our mistakes. We feel ashamed and guilty, which makes us not want to think about them. Unfortunately, this can lead you back into the arms of a narcissist and a toxic relationship.

Instead of feeling bad about your mistakes, do your best to tell yourself it's okay. You can even write the following phrase down and repeat it to yourself often, "I make mistakes just like everyone else. It's okay to make mistakes as they help you learn and grow as a person. It's a way that I can reach my best self."

When you are looking into your toxic relationship, think of the mistakes you made that got you to fall in love with the person. Write this information down and review it often as you work toward feeling better about making mistakes. Furthermore, reminding yourself of the steps that led to the toxic relationship will help you become more aware of the red flags.

Getting Back Into the Right Mindset

ANOTHER PREVENTION technique is to get yourself into the right mindset. You want to have a positive mindset and this will give you a positive self-image and increase your self-worth. This is something you will need to work on in time, especially when you are healing. Focusing on a positive mindset will also help with your healing process as you will start to focus on the positive aspects within your life.

Meditation

IF YOU DON'T MEDITATE, you should try to find the time. It only takes around 10 minutes and you will start to feel the benefits, such as a positive mindset, immediately. Not only can meditation help erase the negativity within you, but it can help you focus on the positives. You can look into mindful meditation, when is when you use a breathing technique in order to get yourself to focus on the present moment. All you need to do is follow a few simple steps:

1. Set aside time every day to meditate. This can be done in the morning to help clear your mind for the day.
2. Find a comfortable place in your home. You might lay or sit down on your couch. No matter where you go, you want to make sure you are comfortable. If you find yourself uncomfortable during meditation, this will take your mind away from the task.
3. Start by clearing your mind. You might want to do this through soothing meditation music or through breathing. If you choose breathing, start by breathing normally. Close your eyes, lay one hand on your stomach, and the other hand on your chest. Focus on your breathing or on the way your hands move as you are breathing. Don't focus on what you need to get done that day, what your emotions are, or anything else. Focus on how relaxing your breathing is.
4. Take several deep and slow breaths. Continue to focus on the present moment and how you are relaxed. If you find your mind wandering, simply bring your attention back to your breathing. Be gentle with

yourself, minds wander. There is nothing wrong with this.
5. Some people like to focus on releasing their negative energy as they bring in positive energy. You can do this by imagining your negative energy leaving your body starting with your toes. The energy moves through your feet, into your ankles, legs, hips, stomach, chest, neck, head, and then out your body. You can then imagine the positive energy in your environment coming into your body in the same way. The energy starts at your toes and works its way throughout your body.
6. Another way to get rid of your negative energy is to imagine it leaving your body every time you exhale. As you inhale, you can then imagine bringing positive energy into your body.
7. After a few minutes or when you feel relaxed, open your eyes and continue with your day.

Focus on the Positive

ANOTHER GREAT WAY TO get into a positive mindset is to focus on the positive. It doesn't matter how small the situation is, what matters is the positivity it brings into your life. For example, you might feel positive when you find $20 in your pants pocket. You might also feel positive when you are able to complete your tasks within a certain time frame. You can even set daily goals which will allow you to focus on how you accomplished your goals at the end of the day.

Turn Negative Self-Talk into Positive Self-Talk

WE ALL TALK AND THINK about ourselves negatively from time to time. Unfortunately, after a toxic relationship, negative self-talk and thinking is going to drastically increase. When you continue to talk about yourself in a negative way, you continue to give the narcissist control over your emotions. Even if they are not there, you are letting the way the treated you affect you. Of course, it is going to take time to change your mindset. But if you don't take control of your thinking, you will continue to allow them to have control.

When you start to talk about yourself in a negative way, change your words. For instance, for every negative comment you make about yourself, give yourself two positive comments. Do the same for any negative thinking. You can also take this a step further and write positive comments about yourself on sticky notes and post them around your home. Allow yourself to see these notes every day as they will help you focus on a positive mindset.

Conclusion

"EMPATHS DID NOT COME into this world to be victims, we came to be warriors. Be brave. Stay strong. We need all hands on deck." - Anthon St. Maarten (Walter, 2019).

It's true, you can often feel like a victim as an empath. This doesn't make you a narcissist, it tells you that you are struggling to find your positive mindset. You are struggling to find your place in this world. While you will probably feel alone with these thoughts, you are not. Every empath goes through these feelings at some point in their lifetime. I know I did. In fact, I will still struggle with them from time to time. I will sometimes catch myself thinking, "Why do I have to be so sensitive?" Sometimes our empath gift does feel more like a curse. It's important to acknowledge this feeling as it will help you grow as an empath. Furthermore, it will allow you to heal from a toxic relationship.

Narcissists and empaths have a magnetic force. It is usually the empath who is the first person to notice the narcissist. At first, they might not want anything to do with you. However, as you continue to give them your attention, they will start to see you as someone they can use. They will become attracted to your emotional field as they are able to feed off your emotions. They are able to gain your sympathy when they have the pity me attitude. They are able to get you to talk about them in high esteem because you don't want to talk negatively about anyone, especially someone you are falling in love with.

Narcissists are able to control you through your emotions. They are able to focus on your negative emotions, such as guilt, which will make you bend and give them what they want. This might include you changing certain pieces of your personality to fit their mold. It could even be that you leave your career and stay home as this is one of the best ways they can control you.

Empaths are givers and narcissists are takers. This is the main reason the two become a pair. Whatever you have, the narcissist wants as it will give them what they want. You will give them attention by focusing on them. As an empath, you are a great listener. You will listen to every word the narcissist says, especially in the beginning when you feel there is love. You will also want to make them feel good about themselves because that is what you do. For example, when they come to you and act like a victim due to a mistake they made, you are going to do what you can to make them feel better. You might agree with them as they blame someone else for their mistake. You might tell them about their great qualities.

Then, without you noticing it, the narcissist will start to feed off your energy. Empaths hold a lot of positive energy because they strive to make people feel better. Even if you are suffering with your own problems at the moment, you are able to put this aside and focus on helping the person in front of you. When you do this with a narcissist, they will suck the positive energy out of you. This will make you feel emotionally and psychologically drained. You won't understand why you feel this way, at least not at first. However, the more you pay attention to your surroundings, the more you will be able to see what the narcissist is doing to you.

This book went beyond the steps of healing from a toxic relationship. It brought you to the beginning. It showed you how you get caught in a toxic relationship time and time again. This book gave you information on what narcissism is, so you can gain a better understanding of the person and watch for red flags. Understanding will be able to keep you from falling into another toxic relationship. You also learned a bit about yourself as an empath. Not everyone is aware of the power their empathic abilities hold, which can also lead us into one toxic relationship after the other. Furthermore, to understand the magnetic pull between empaths and narcissists, you need to have a clear understanding of both personalities.

There are many factors I want you to take away from this book. I want you to know that you hold a special gift that allows you to truly heal people. At the same time, you need to be aware of who you are trying to heal. Not everyone wants their emotional wounds to heal. I also want you to know that you can help someone who doesn't want your help. People need to want to help themselves before they will allow anyone else to help them. But, the most important message is understanding the give and take between empaths and narcissists, so you don't find yourself in another toxic relationship. Remember, you are not alone in this world. There are millions of empathic people who are going through the same situation. Take time to heal and know your self-worth.

If you enjoyed this book, remember to check out the companion books in the series! EMPATH AWAKENING, a book that will help you stop absorbing hurtful emotions from others, AM I CODEPENDENT?, about an affliction that many empaths find themselves coping with, and INVSISIBLE ABUSE, about the covert abuse narcissists can deal out to empaths, sensitive people, and others. All three are available where you purchased this title, written by me, Kara Lawrence! These books are also available on audio to listen to.

Have you learned something useful or enjoyed reading? Please consider leaving a review! This is a big help to me in putting out more books like this one. Thank you, and good luck on your relationship journey!

References

10 STEPS TO GETTING Your Life Back After Narcissistic Abuse. (2017). Retrieved 29 August 2019, from https://medium.com/@SoulGPS/10-steps-to-getting-your-life-back-after-narcissistic-abuse-96b5c74af29c

Androff, B. (2019). Why Empaths & Narcissists Are Attracted To Each Other (And The Toxic Relationship Between Them). Retrieved 28 August 2019, from https://www.yourtango.com/2018314308/toxic-relationship-between-empath-and-narcissist-attraction

Borchard, T. (2018). You Deplete Me: 10 Steps to End a Toxic Relationship. Retrieved 29 August 2019, from https://psychcentral.com/blog/you-deplete-me-10-steps-to-end-a-toxic-relationship/

Bryan, K. (2019). 25 Inspirational Quotes to Help You End Your Toxic Relationship. Retrieved 31 August 2019, from https://pairedlife.com/breakups/25-Inspirational-Quotes-to-Help-You-End-Your-Toxic-Relationship

Daskal, L. (2016). 35 Signs You're in a Toxic Relationship. Retrieved 27 August 2019, from https://www.inc.com/lolly-daskal/35-signs-youre-in-a-toxic-business-relationship.html

Dodgson, L. Empaths and narcissists make a 'toxic' partnership — here's why they're attracted to each other. Retrieved 28 August 2019, from https://www.businessinsider.com/why-empaths-and-narcissists-are-attracted-to-each-other-2018-1

Energy Vampires Quiz. Retrieved 28 August 2019, from https://psychcentral.com/quizzes/energy-vampires-quiz/

Energy Vampires: 8 Signs and Symptoms To Look Out For. Retrieved 28 August 2019, from https://www.psychicgurus.org/8-signs-you-might-be-an-energy-vampire/

Fon, R. 7 Of The Most Harmful Narcissistic Manipulation Tactics. Retrieved 30 August 2019, from https://iheartintelligence.com/7-narcissistic-manipulation/

Fox, R. (2015). The 32 Traits of an Empath. Retrieved 28 August 2019, from https://blog.thewellnessuniverse.com/32-traits-empath/

Fuller, K. (2018). Overcoming the Aftermath of Leaving a Toxic Relationship. Retrieved 29 August 2019, from https://www.psychologytoday.com/us/blog/happiness-is-state-mind/201805/overcoming-the-aftermath-leaving-toxic-relationship

Gilbert, B. (2016). Do You Have a Codependent Personality?. Retrieved 30 August 2019, from https://www.everydayhealth.com/emotional-health/do-you-have-a-codependent-personality.aspx

Greenberg, E. (2018). How to Avoid Toxic Relationships. Retrieved 30 August 2019, from https://www.psychologytoday.com/us/blog/understanding-narcissism/201807/how-avoid-toxic-relationships

Holland, K. (2018). How to Recognize and Respond to Energy Vampires at Home, Work, and More. Retrieved 29 August 2019, from https://www.healthline.com/health/mental-health/energy-vampires

Kassel, G. (2019). 11 Signs You're Dating a Narcissist — and How to Deal with Them. Retrieved 28 August 2019, from https://www.healthline.com/health/mental-health/am-i-dating-a-narcissist#1

Lancer, D. (2018). Symptoms of Codependency. Retrieved 30 August 2019, from https://psychcentral.com/lib/symptoms-of-codependency/

Love, L. (2019). 13 Signs You have Energy Vampires in Your Life. Retrieved 29 August 2019, from https://www.fineminds.com/happiness/13-signs-that-youre-being-drained-dry/

Luna, A. 27 Signs of a Toxic Relationship (Everything You Need to Know). Retrieved 28 August 2019, from https://lonerwolf.com/toxic-relationships/

Luna, A. Dear Empaths: 4 Types of Narcissists You May Be Attracting. Retrieved 28 August 2019, from https://lonerwolf.com/empaths-and-narcissists/

Malkin, C. (2013). 5 Early Warning Signs You're With a Narcissist. Retrieved 27 August 2019, from https://www.psychologytoday.com/us/blog/romance-redux/201306/5-early-warning-signs-youre-narcissist

Meyers, S. (2012). Loving Broken Men: Rescuing Mr. Potential, Part 1. Retrieved 29 August 2019, from https://www.psychologytoday.com/us/blog/insight-is-2020/201207/loving-broken-men-rescuing-mr-potential-part-1

Milstead, K. The Emotional Hell of Going No Contact with a Narcissist. Retrieved 30 August 2019, from https://fairytaleshadows.com/emotional-hell-going-no-contact-with-a-narcissist/

NerdLove. (2016). Enforcing Your Boundaries. Retrieved 30 August 2019, from https://www.doctornerdlove.com/enforcing-your-boundaries/

Neuharth, D. (2017). 11 Ways to Set Boundaries with Narcissists. Retrieved 31 August 2019, from https://blogs.psychcentral.com/narcissism-decoded/2017/06/11-ways-to-set-boundaries-with-narcissists/

Ni, P. (2019). 7 Ways Narcissists Manipulate Relationships. Retrieved 31 August 2019, from https://www.psychologytoday.com/us/blog/communication-success/201903/7-ways-narcissists-manipulate-relationships

Ni, P. (2014). 10 Signs That You're in a Relationship with a Narcissist. Retrieved 28 August 2019, from https://www.psychologytoday.com/us/blog/communication-success/201409/10-signs-youre-in-relationship-narcissist

Orloff, J. Could You Be in Love with an Energy Vampire?. Retrieved 30 August 2019, from https://drjudithorloff.com/could-you-be-in-love-with-an-energy-vampire-video/

Schoenwald, C. (2016). You Can't Fix Somebody Who Doesn't Want To Be Fixed. Retrieved 29 August 2019, from https://www.yourtango.com/2016286163/why-was-only-attracted-damaged-men

Stages of Recovery after Narcissist Abuse. Retrieved 29 August 2019, from https://narcissistabusesupport.com/stages-of-grief-after-narcissist-abuse/

Walter, A. (2019). 50 inspiring quotes for highly sensitive people and empaths. Retrieved 31 August 2019, from https://hisensitives.com/50-inspiring-quotes-for-highly-sensitive-people-and-empaths/

Wright, M. 21 Stages Of The Relationship Between A Narcissist And An Empath. Retrieved 30 August 2019, from https://thepowerofsilence.co/21-stages-of-the-relationship-between-a-narcissist-and-an-empath/

Youssef, E. (2016). Dear Selfless Women, This is Why we Attract Men who Need Fixing. Retrieved 30 August 2019, from https://www.elephantjournal.com/2016/02/dear-self-less-women-this-is-why-we-attract-men-who-need-fixing/

Z, S. (2018). Why Empaths Tend To Attract Narcissist Partners. Retrieved 28 August 2019, from https://www.7thsensepsychics.com/stories/empaths-tend-attract-narcissist-partners/

www.ingramcontent.com/pod-product-compliance
Lightning Source LLC
Chambersburg PA
CBHW052059110526
44591CB00013B/2277